Andrew Edney

Netbooks

In easy steps is an imprint of In Easy Steps Limited
Southfield Road · Southam
Warwickshire CV47 0FB · United Kingdom
www.ineasysteps.com

Notice of Liability
Every effort has been made to ensure that this book contains accurate
and current information. However, In Easy Steps Limited and the
author shall not be liable for any loss or damage suffered by readers
as a result of any information contained herein.

Trademarks
Microsoft® and Windows® are registered trademarks of Microsoft
Corporation. All other trademarks are acknowledged as belonging to
their respective companies.

In Easy Steps Limited supports The Forest Stewardship Council (FSC),
the leading international forest certification organisation. All our titles
that are printed on Greenpeace approved FSC certified paper carry the
FSC logo.

Mixed Sources
Product group from well-managed
forests and other controlled sources
www.fsc.org Cert no. SGS-COC-005998
© 1996 Forest Stewardship Council

Printed and bound in the United Kingdom

ISBN 978-1-84078-390-2

Contents

6 Home Networking 91

7 Going Online 109

12 Pictures and Photos

13 Watching TV

14 Securing Your Netbook

Index   **209**

1 Netbooks

This chapter will introduce netbooks and will explain what a netbook is, why you might want one and various other things including how to carry your netbook and how to upgrade it.

What is a Netbook?

Netbooks are a fairly new addition to the computer family. They are small, light and inexpensive computers that are designed to carry out selected tasks, such as browsing the Internet, catching up on emails, doing some work and more. They are not designed to be like the powerhouse laptops and desktops that can pretty much do anything, but are instead designed to be additions to those items of kit if needed.

Netbooks are sometimes referred to as mini notebooks or even subnotebooks.

Because netbooks are smaller and lighter than most laptops, they tend to have lower specifications than their big brothers. This reduced specification is usually found in the processor or the memory, and sometimes in the number of ports on the netbook. It also means that there is no DVD optical drive built into the netbook, although that certainly doesn't stop you from adding one yourself later.

Don't be put off by the reduced specifications though as they are more than adequate to do the tasks you would need a netbook to perform.

The first netbook was introduced in 2007 when a company called ASUS released the ASUS Eee PC. It weighed about 2lb and had a 7-inch display. It didn't take long for companies such as MSI, Dell and HP to release their own netbooks.

Hot tip

There are a lot of really good deals to be had on netbooks – you can even get them for free in certain situations from companies like your mobile phone provider.

Initially a lot of people saw netbooks as a bit of a gimmick – they looked nice, but they just didn't have the computing power of a normal laptop or desktop. Eventually this perception problem disappeared when people realized that their reduced size and performance meant that the battery life was increased, they were easy to carry in a bag, and they could be used anywhere. Today for example, some netbooks claim to have batteries that will last for nine hours or more, which means even the most hardened traveller can use their netbook anywhere without the need to carry the power supply or worry about the battery running out too quickly.

A typical netbook specification includes:

- A 9- or 10-inch display (anything more than about 10 inches would probably be seen as a laptop rather than a netbook)

- Wireless internet connectivity

- A low powered processor (currently most are based on the Intel Atom chipset running at 1.6 GHz)

- Long battery life (depending on the battery pack)

- At least one USB port

- 1GB RAM

- 160GB Hard Drive (although this really does depend on the model and specification of the netbook)

- Weight of around 2lb to 3lb

- Built-in webcam

Obviously while that may be a typical specification for a netbook, there are netbooks out there that have a much lower specification and also those that have a significantly higher specification. The difference in specification tends to come down to price. If you don't need a certain feature, for example you don't require a large hard drive, then you may save yourself some money by opting for a lower specification netbook.

Don't worry though as most netbooks are upgradable, and this will be covered later in this chapter and is fairly easy to do.

Hot tip

When you are looking at netbooks make sure that you look at the specifications whilst considering exactly what you want to use it for. For example, if you want to use it a lot whilst travelling you will probably want a netbook with a larger capacity battery.

Hot tip

When choosing a netbook you might want to consider looking at slightly older models as they will be even cheaper and the spec may still meet your needs.

Why a Netbook?

So you might be asking yourself why you may want to consider buying a netbook given the "limitations" of having a slower processor, no DVD drive, and so on.

Perhaps the following will help you to decide:

- Netbooks are small and light and so are very easy to carry around in a bag or case

- Depending on the netbook, the battery life is fantastic and can last you for multiple journeys between each charge

- If you only want to do certain tasks, such as checking your email, communicating with friends, listening to music, surfing the Internet or just catching up on a bit of work when you are out and about, netbooks are perfect

- Netbooks are inexpensive computers compared to some desktops and laptops – there are a lot of very good value netbooks to be found

- Netbooks can be considerably smaller than laptops

- They will run Windows 7 very well, even better than Windows Vista

- Netbooks are not replacements for desktops or even laptops – they are additions that have their place

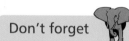

Don't forget

Because a netbook has less processing power than a laptop or desktop, it is not really designed for playing graphic intensive games or for heavy processing like video conversion.

Netbook Terminology

If you are new to netbooks (and possibly even to computers) then some of the terminology that is used might sound a little alien to you. Here are some terms that you might want to know:

- **Processor** - also known as a CPU (Central Processing Unit). The processor is the heart of your netbook. The better the processor, the more you can do with your netbook and the faster it will operate

- **Memory** - also known as RAM (Random Access Memory). The more memory that your netbook has the more programs can be run and the faster it will operate

- **Hard Drive** - also known as storage. The hard drive is what is used to store the programs you want to run on your netbook along with any data, such as music or pictures you want to keep. The larger the hard drive, the more data storage you have available to use. Think of it as a giant filing cabinet

- **Connectivity** - this refers to the types of things that can be connected to your netbook, such as USB devices, camera memory cards and other things

- **Graphics card** - this is a device that is used to display images on the netbook screen. The more powerful the graphics card the better the quality that is displayed on the screen

- **Wireless** - this is the capability of the netbook to connect to, and use, a wireless network for accessing services such as the Internet

- **Ports** - these are the connectors on the netbook, such as USB ports, headphone ports, etc.

- **Webcam** - this is a device that is built into your netbook that enables you to have video conversations with other people using applications like Windows Live Messenger or Skype. You can also use it to take still pictures as well. If your netbook doesn't have a webcam built in you can buy one and connect it via USB

- **Trackpad/Pointer** - each netbook comes with a trackpad or pointer. By simply using your finger you are able to control the cursor on the screen

Hot tip

All of the terms on this page will be covered in greater detail in later chapters.

Ports on the Netbook

If you have a close look at a netbook you will see a number of different ports and connectors around it. These ports and connectors are used to connect a variety of different devices to your netbook to enable you to be able to use them.

These ports and connectors may include:

- **USB** - all netbooks will have at least one USB port for connecting USB devices such as mice, printers and external CD/DVD rewriters

- **Ethernet port** - this is the network port and is used to connect an Ethernet network cable so that you can use your netbook on a wired network

- **Monitor port** - used to connect your netbook to an external monitor

- **Memory card port** - used to plug a camera memory card directly into the netbook in order to view, copy and edit your digital photographs

- **Headphone and microphone sockets** - used to connect headphones and a microphone for media related tasks

- **Power socket** - used to connect a power supply to your netbook for charging and using directly from the mains

- **Kensington lock** - used to secure your netbook to a lock for security purposes to stop it from being stolen

Hot tip

If you don't think that you have enough USB ports on your netbook, you can buy a USB port replicator.

Don't forget

Not all netbooks have the same ports and connectors so your netbook might not have everything listed here but it also might have something not listed!

14

Wireless Access

In the not too distant past, the only way to connect to a network or the Internet was via wires, whether that was via network cables or via modem cables. The same was true for printers.

Then along came wireless technology and it does exactly what it says – it removes the need for wires.

This meant that all of a sudden you didn't need to carry a whole mess of wires around with you if you wanted to connect.

Wireless gives you the capability to connect your netbook to various wireless networks and devices.

There are two main components needed to connect to a wireless device – the wireless device itself, whether that is a wireless router, a wireless access point or a wireless printer, and a wireless card.

All netbooks come with wireless cards built in – if one doesn't then you really should pick another netbook.

Types of wireless networks and devices include:

- Wireless access points and hotspots
- Wireless networks at home or at work
- Wireless devices such as printers and storage devices

Wireless Access Points and Hotspots

If you are using your netbook when you are on the go, then there is a good chance that at some point you will want to connect to the Internet, whether it is to check your email, surf the Internet or any number of other tasks that you need to be connected for. To do this you will need to first connect your netbook to a wireless access point or hotspot. These are available in a number of public locations including:

- Hotels
- Airports
- Coffee Shops
- Libraries

Some are free and some you need to pay for. For example, some coffee shops will provide wireless access if you buy their coffee.

Hot tip

For more information on wireless, how to configure it and how to use it, see Chapter 8 later in the book.

Beware

When connecting to a wireless hotspot or in a hotel, you should be careful about what you do on your netbook unless you are sure of the security offered by the wireless provider.

15

For more information on batteries take a look at Chapter 3.

Accessories

There are a number of accessories and even spares that you should consider getting for use with your netbook – whether you are on the go a lot, or even if you just use your netbook at home. Whether these accessories are essential items – or just nice to have items – is entirely down to you and what your needs are.

Accessories and spares that you should consider buying are:

● **Spare battery** – depending on how much you travel and want to use your netbook without external power, and the type of battery you have, you might want a spare battery

● **Power cable** – you will have one already with your netbook, but you might want to consider a spare if you use your netbook in more than one location

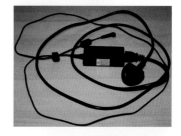

● **Mouse** – using the trackpad on your netbook can sometimes be tricky so having a mouse can help. You can buy wired, wireless or even bluetooth mice

● **External CD/DVD Rewriter** – as netbooks don't have a built-in CD or DVD rewriter you will need to get one if you want to watch films, listen to music, load additional software and write CDs or DVDs

- **USB pen drives** – always a useful addition as you can use them to copy data to and from your netbook and another computer. You can also use them for data storage, including music

- **External hard drives** – similar to USB pen drives only significantly greater in available data size, external hard drives are additionally useful for data backups and storing lots of data that you may not want on your netbook all the time

> **Hot tip**
>
> If you do a lot of travelling and you want to watch movies or listen to music in comfort you should consider buying a pair of noise-canceling headphones.

- **Headphones** – if you plan on listening to music or watching movies on your netbook whilst on the go then you should consider headphones, not only for you but for the sake of those around you. Other people are probably not interested in listening to your music and movies

- **Printer** – there will come a time when you will probably want to print something out – maybe a Word document or maybe a photograph, in which case you will need a printer. Depending on what you might want to print on the go, there are different size printers

> **Hot tip**
>
> For information on how to connect various devices to your netbook take a look at Chapter 4.

17

Using the Keyboard

Netbooks have the same style of keyboard as that found on laptops and desktops. The biggest difference is that of the size of the keyboard – a netbook keyboard is usually a lot smaller.

Because of the size difference in the keyboard it can take a little while to get used to using it while you retrain your fingers if you are already used to using a keyboard – it is very easy to press the wrong keys because you are used to them being in a slightly different place.

Another major difference between a netbook keyboard and a desktop keyboard is the mouse pad or trackpad that can be found below the keyboard of a netbook.

Don't forget

If you are not comfortable when you are using the keyboard then try repositioning your hands and wrists and see if that helps.

This mouse pad or trackpad is used to move the cursor around the screen and also to select things. It can be very sensitive and it is easy to knock if you are not holding your fingers correctly.

The hands and wrists should be kept in a straight wrist posture when typing:

Ergonomic Advice

As you will be using your netbook in a variety of different locations, and probably for extended periods of time, it is vital that you sit in the correct position when you use your netbook and also that you position the screen correctly.

This may sound obvious but a lot of people don't do it and they experience discomfort with prolonged use of their netbook.

Because of a netbook's small size, users could be forced into awkward postures. What can happen is that the screen may be positioned correctly but the keyboard is then at an awkward angle and vice versa.

The Best Seating Position

If you are sitting at a desk using your netbook, then the best seating position is as follows:

- Your neck aligned with your spine (not bent or thrust forward)

- Your back relaxed but supported by a good chair

- Your shoulders relaxed (not hunched or rounded)

- Your elbows close to your body and bent at an angle between 90 and 120 degrees

- Your wrists and hands straight (not bent or turned)

Hot tip

The best place to use your netbook is at a desk or other flat surface.

The ideal type of chair is an office type chair – basically one you would expect to find in an office – one that is designed with good posture in mind. If you don't have one of those then any chair with a straight back can be used.

Netbook Position

It is very important that wherever you use your netbook, both the keyboard and screen can be used without you being uncomfortable.

Do not have the netbook too low or too high otherwise you will need to strain to reach it and that will soon cause you discomfort and worse still over time could cause you an injury.

Hot tip

For more information on using an external monitor, see Chapter 4 later in the book.

Netbook Screen Position

The position of the netbook screen is very important. With a desktop computer you have the screen at eye level but this is not possible with a netbook.

The best position is to tilt the netbook screen so that it is perpendicular to your line of sight as long as the lighting permits.

Beware

Do not place your netbook on a pillow or other soft material as it may reduce the air circulation which in turn will make your netbook very hot and could damage it.

Lighting can actually be a big problem with netbooks as the screen can reflect glare from either sunlight or from indoor lighting. The way to reduce this is to change your position if you can or to close a curtain or blind if one is available. Whatever happens you should not sit and squint at the screen as you will suffer from eyestrain.

Hot tip

Always ensure that your netbook screen is clean and free from dust in order to reduce viewing problems.

Other Tips

There are a number of other useful tips that you can use in order to help you:

- If you are using your netbook for prolonged periods of time, you should try and take frequent short breaks

- Consider using an external monitor if you can – this will help reduce the risk of eyestrain

- Consider using an external mouse instead of the built-in trackpad to reduce wrist fatigue

- Try not to use your netbook directly on your lap as it may get hot and you could burn yourself – you may want to consider using a tray or other flat object to rest the netbook on

- Consider using a cushion for extra support and comfort if you are going to be seated for a long period of time

- Adjust the height on your chair if you can to make your seating position as comfortable as possible

Carrying Your Netbook

Unless you plan on only ever using your netbook in one location, you are going to need to carry it around from place to place. Even though one of the major features of netbooks is their minimal weight, after a period of time carrying it, it can become uncomfortable. Add to the netbook its power supply, any accessories and anything else you might need to carry, you will need to make sure you carry everything correctly.

There are a couple of fairly obvious points to remember when carrying your netbook:

● Carry the netbook around in a specially designed and correctly sized netbook carry case

● Carry the netbook around on one side of your body and if you are beginning to find it uncomfortable change to the other side

Beware

As netbooks are prime targets for theft, you should always be aware of your surroundings.

● Don't overload the bag with unnecessary items

● Don't carry more things than you can safely manage

● If you are becoming tired, stop and have a rest

● Whatever bag you use make sure the strap is padded

Selecting a Carry Case

Selecting a carry case is probably more important than you might think. This is what you will be carrying your netbook and any accessories around in so it has to be perfect for you. Some people just use a normal bag or briefcase, but there are numerous advantages to using a proper carry case:

- They are designed specifically to transport a netbook

- They will be more comfortable to carry your netbook and accessories around in

- They look good

Selecting the right size case is also very important. You want the case to be large enough to fit your netbook and accessories in but you don't want it to be so big that the netbook will move around when carrying the case and possibly be damaged.

Here are two main types of case you should consider:

Carry Case

The carry case, or bag, is the traditional choice. This is designed specifically to carry your netbook and any accessories around, and also, depending on the size of the bag, other items such as books.

Sleeve

A netbook sleeve is designed to fit around your netbook and to protect it from damage.

You can buy a sleeve that fits your netbook perfectly and then you can carry the sleeve around separately or in another bag along with your accessories.

Hot tip

Decide just how much you will be carrying around and choose an appropriate bag. If you think that you will only ever be carrying around the netbook then consider a smaller bag.

Upgrading the Memory

Chances are that your netbook doesn't have the maximum amount of memory (RAM) pre-installed. This means that for a small amount of money you can upgrade or replace the existing memory which will make your netbook run faster and perform better.

Replacing or upgrading the memory only takes a few minutes but before you start you will need to check how much memory is already in the netbook and what the maximum amount of memory is that the netbook can take. All this information should be available on the manufacturer's website. For example, your netbook probably came with 1GB of memory and can take a maximum of 2GB of memory.

Before you buy any new memory you should check to see if you can add an additional piece of memory or if you have to replace what is already there with a new piece.

Once you have found all this out and purchased the new memory, perform the following to replace what is already there:

1 Ensure the netbook is switched off and anything attached is removed, and then turn it upside down

2 Locate the panel that holds the memory and take a small screwdriver to carefully remove the screw

3 Gently lift the panel open and remove it, being careful not to bend or break it

Hot tip

If your netbook has a free memory slot then you can add memory rather than replacing it, in which case just skip steps 4 and 5.

4 Locate the clips either side of the memory that are holding it in place and gently push them away from the memory. This should release the memory from the clip

5 Carefully slide out the memory by holding it with your finger and your thumb and pulling it away from the slot

6 Take the new piece of memory and slot it in by putting it in at an angle and then pressing down carefully until it clicks into place and the clips are holding it firmly

7 Replace the panel and the screw

8 Switch on the netbook and confirm it can see the new memory

Hot tip

To see how much memory you have in your netbook, see Basic Computer Information in Chapter 5.

25

Upgrading the Hard Drive

Depending on which netbook you have, you may want to consider upgrading the hard drive to give you more space for programs and your data, such as music and photographs. There are different types of hard drives that offer all sorts of capacity.

The two most popular hard drives on netbooks today are 2.5" SATA drives and SSD drives.

2.5" SATA Drives

These are the most common drives found in netbooks (and also laptops). They come in a variety of different capacities so take a look at what size you really need. SATA stands for Serial Advanced Technology Attachment and refers to the type of attachment on the drive itself.

To replace a 2.5" SATA drive:

Beware

Make sure that you buy the correct type of hard drive for your netbook. If you are in any doubt consult the documentation that came with your netbook or contact the manufacturer.

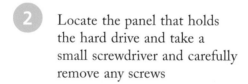

1 Ensure the netbook is switched off and anything attached is removed, and then turn it upside down

2 Locate the panel that holds the hard drive and take a small screwdriver and carefully remove any screws

3 Carefully lift up and remove the cover from the back of the netbook ensuring that you do not use too much force to remove it

Beware

This is not a simple case of just swapping out the hard drive – you will need to then completely reinstall Windows and the software you had installed once you finish the upgrade. So if you are in any doubt about how to do this, you might want to reconsider.

4 Locate any screws holding the hard drive in place and remove them carefully

5 Slide the hard drive out of the drive bay and carefully lift up ensuring you do not use too much force to remove it

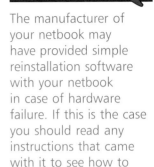

6 Place the hard drive on a clean flat surface and locate the screws on the drive enclosure holding the hard drive in place then remove them carefully

7 Slide the hard drive out of the hard drive enclosure and replace it with the new hard drive

8 Replace the screws and carefully refit the hard drive back into the netbook, ensure all screws are replaced

9 Reinstall the operating system and any applications that you need – if you are in any doubt about how to do this, consult the manual that came with your netbook

SSD Drives

SSD stands for Solid State Disk and is the latest in hard drive technology. They have no moving parts so are faster and quieter, but they are also more expensive and do not yet have the same capacity as SATA hard drives.

Some netbooks use a type of SSD drive with a mini PCI-e slot, which just describes the type of connector the drive uses to connect to the netbook, in the same way as a SATA drive uses a SATA connector to connect.

...cont'd

If your netbook does have one of these SSD drives in it you will notice that it actually looks a bit like a memory chip rather than a hard drive as it is very thin.

To replace an SSD drive:

1. Ensure the netbook is switched off and anything attached is removed, and then turn it upside down

2. Locate the panel that holds the SSD drive then take a small screwdriver and carefully remove any screws

3. Carefully lift up and remove the cover from the back of the netbook ensuring that you do not use too much force to remove it

4. Locate any screws holding the SSD drive in place and remove them

5. Carefully remove the existing SSD drive

6. Carefully insert the new SSD drive into the slot

7. Put all the screws back into place and refit the panel

8. Reinstall the operating system and any applications that you need – if you are in any doubt about how to do this, consult the manual that came with your netbook

Keeping Your Netbook Clean

Keeping your netbook clean helps to ensure that it doesn't get damaged and that it is in the best possible condition. Like anything else, if it is kept clean and is well looked after, it will last longer. The two main areas you need to keep clean are the screen and the keyboard area.

Cleaning the Screen

You may be surprised just how quickly dirt, dust and fingerprints accumulate on your netbook screen. Over time this makes it harder to read and could cause you problems.

You can clean the screen with the following:

- A lint-free cloth

- A cleaning solution designed for computer screens or TV screens

- Screen wipes

Cleaning the Keyboard

Like the screen, the keyboard can get dirty very quickly, and you will often find bits of dust, crumbs, food and other things between the keys. A good way to clean the keyboard is to buy a can of compressed air and gently spray the keyboard until all the dirt and dust has gone.

Beware

Never clean your netbook with a wet cloth. You can use a damp cloth but make sure it is not too wet and never use any sort of soap product.

Hot tip

You should clean your netbook on a regular basis – this includes the screen and also the keyboard – you may be surprised just how much dirt and dust can get between the keys.

Beware

Always read the instructions on the compressed air canister – and be careful as prolonged use makes the canister very cold!

Windows 7 Editions

Windows 7 is the latest and greatest desktop operating system from Microsoft. There are four different editions of Microsoft Windows 7:

- Windows 7 Starter
- Windows 7 Home Premium
- Windows 7 Professional
- Windows 7 Ultimate

There are also 32-bit and 64-bit editions of Windows 7.

Most netbooks will come pre-installed with either Windows 7 Starter edition or Windows 7 Home Premium edition.

Windows 7 Starter
Windows 7 Starter edition contains everything you will need to get started, including:

- Built-in security including Windows Defender and Windows Firewall so you can be protected very quickly and easily

Windows 7 Home Premium
Windows 7 Home Premium edition contains everything you will need to get an enhanced user experience, including:

- Built-in security including Windows Defender and Windows Firewall so you can be protected very quickly and easily
- Windows Media Center
- The new Windows Aero user interface
- Built-in DVD and CD authoring facilities
- Enhanced Windows Mobility and support
- Homegroups for easier sharing of information throughout your home network

Hot tip

If you want to be able to do more with your netbook then just the very basics, you will want to use Windows 7 Home Premium edition.

Beware

If your netbook is currently running Windows XP then you cannot upgrade directly to Windows 7 – you will need to perform a clean installation and reinstall your programs and data.

2 Exploring Your Netbook

This chapter will guide you around your netbook, showing you how to open it, connect it to the power, start and shut down and even make some adjustments so it is easier to use.

Opening it up

The first thing you need to do in order to use your netbook is to open it up. Netbooks have a clamshell design which means that the screen and the keyboard are together when closed and are only accessible when pulled apart.

1 To open the netbook, place your hand on the lid and lift upwards

2 When the lid is open and the screen is visible, move the screen into a position that will be comfortable for you to see and use

The screen should stay in whatever position you place it.

Connecting the Power

The next thing you should do is to connect the power supply to the netbook, unless of course you are planning on using it from the battery.

1 Ensure that the power supply is connected securely to the mains power

Hot tip

Depending on your netbook, the power port could be on the left hand side, the right hand side or even on the back – so find where yours is located.

2 Carefully push the power connector into the power port

Beware

Do not apply too much force when connecting the power connector to the netbook otherwise you might damage either or both of them.

3 Switch the power on at the mains

Switching it on

Now that you are ready to use your netbook, you need to switch it on. Most netbooks have the on/off switch located above the keyboard.

Hot tip

Depending on your netbook, the on/off switch could be on the left hand side, the right hand side or even on the keyboard itself.

To switch on the netbook, just press the on/off button firmly and then let go. If you hold down the button for too long then it is likely to shut itself back off instead of booting up.

You will hear a noise coming from the netbook when it is powering up – this could include a beep or chime, and also the sound of the hard drive spinning up.

Once the netbook has completed loading the operating system, the starting screen should be displayed. You can now start using your netbook.

Don't forget

Your netbook will take a short while to boot up and be ready for you to start using it.

The Start Button

The single most powerful button in Windows 7 is the Start button. The Start button is what launches the Start menu and from there you can start applications such as an Internet browser, shut down your netbook, configure hardware like printers and much more.

The Start button can be found in the bottom left hand corner of the screen:

If you click on it, the Start menu will appear in the bottom left hand part of the screen and from there you can click on whatever application or menu item that you want.

Hot tip

You will also notice a Windows key on your keyboard. If you press this key it has the same effect as clicking on the Start button.

35

The Start Menu

The Start menu is the place where you can choose which programs you want to run, where you can change any Windows settings, configure any hardware, such as a printer, search for anything on your netbook, shut down your netbook and much more.

Don't forget

Different applications and items will appear on your Start menu depending on how you use your netbook – this is to make life easier for you and how you work.

It is called the Start menu because it is the place where most people will start their activities from.

The Start menu is divided into three main areas.

The large pane on the left hand side of the Start menu shows a list of programs that have either recently been opened or those that have been placed to help you the first few times you use Windows.

Below this left pane is the Search box. This is used to search for programs and files that are stored on your netbook. There is more on Search later in Chapter 5.

Search programs and files

Hot tip

You can add items to the Start menu that you use on a regular basis. You can see how to do that later in Chapter 5.

The large pane on the right hand side of the Start menu gives you easy access to commonly used folders, settings and configuration options.

You will notice that the user name of the person using the netbook is displayed – in this case, Andrew Edney. Under that are shortcuts to my Documents folder, my Pictures folder and my Music folder.

There is also a link to Help and Support.

It also contains the Shut down button for when you are finished using your netbook.

Opening Programs

The most common use of the Start menu is to open programs. Unless you have shortcut icons on your desktop, you will need to start whichever program you want to use from the Start menu. As you have seen on the previous page, recently used programs are shown for ease of access.

Hot tip

You can pin program items to the menu list to make them available all the time – more on this later in Chapter 5.

1 Click on the Start button

2 If the program you want to open is shown in the left pane just click on the icon to open it

All Programs

Obviously not all of the programs you might want to open will be shown in that left pane due to space limitations.

This is where the All Programs link comes in. When you click on it the left hand pane changes to show a list of all available programs and folders, and if you click on a folder, the contents of that folder are also displayed for you to choose from.

1 Click on the Start button

2 Click on the All Programs button

3 Use the scroll bar to move up and down through the list until you find what you are looking for

4 Either click on the program icon you want to open or click on the folder to open it and then click on the program icon you want to open

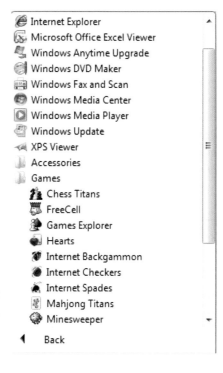

Internet Explorer
Microsoft Office Excel Viewer
Windows Anytime Upgrade
Windows DVD Maker
Windows Fax and Scan
Windows Media Center
Windows Media Player
Windows Update
XPS Viewer
Accessories
Games
    Chess Titans
    FreeCell
    Games Explorer
    Hearts
    Internet Backgammon
    Internet Checkers
    Internet Spades
    Mahjong Titans
    Minesweeper

◀ Back

Hot tip

If you want to know more about a program all you have to do is hover over the name of the program for a detailed description to be shown to you.

Shutting Down

When you have finished using your netbook it is very important that you shut it down correctly in order to ensure your files are safe and that you don't cause any corruption to them. It also saves energy and makes your netbook more secure.

To shut down your netbook:

1 Click on the Start button

2 Click on the Shut down button from the Start menu

When you click Shut down, any open programs will be closed, Windows will then shut down and when that process has completed your netbook display will be off along with the netbook itself. If you have the power supply connected, the netbook will still receive power and will charge its battery if needed.

Sleeping and Hibernation

You could also choose to put your netbook to sleep or even into hibernation. Putting it to sleep turns off the netbook's display and puts it into a low-power state, saving all of your work to memory. This still uses a small amount of power but means that when you restart your netbook everything will look exactly the same as it did before you put the netbook to sleep. Putting your netbook into hibernation is very similar, only hibernation saves all of your work to the netbook's hard drive, which means if the power runs out all of your work is safe.

The reason for using either of these two options is if you want to shut down your netbook but are planning on using it again quickly or if you want to save some extra power.

1 Click on the arrow to the right of the Shut down button

2 Click on either Sleep or Hibernate, depending on which power-save option you want to use

Switch user
Log off
Lock
Restart
Sleep
Hibernate

Depending on how your netbook has been configured, there are also a few other ways to shut down or put it into sleep or hibernation:

● Press (rather than hold down) the power button

● Close the lid

Resuming From Sleep or Hibernation
If you want to use your netbook when it is currently in sleep or hibernation mode, all you need to do is press the netbook power button to wake it up. It is very quick to resume from sleep mode because everything is stored in memory, whereas it is a little slower resuming from hibernation because everything is stored on disk. Both of these however may be quicker than starting your netbook from being powered off completely.

Restarting Your Netbook
If you need to restart your netbook, for example you may have installed some new software, just choose Restart from the menu and your netbook will restart.

Logging Off Your Netbook
If more than one person uses your netbook, or you just want to log off but you don't want to shut down then you can choose the Log off option from the menu. This will close any of your applications and return you to the Log on screen.

Adjusting Screen Resolution

Being able to see the screen clearly and comfortably is very important, even more so on a netbook which has a small screen. Windows does a very good job of choosing the best display settings for you, but if you feel that the screen resolution is not right, then it is fairly simple to change it to something that may be better for you. If you have the wrong settings, it could cause you discomfort.

To change the screen resolution:

Hot tip

The higher the screen resolution, the sharper and clearer the screen will be, but it will be smaller.

1 Click on the Start button

2 Click on Control Panel

3 From the Appearance and Personalization menu, click on Adjust screen resolution

Appearance and Personalization
Change the theme
Change desktop background
Adjust screen resolution

Beware

If you have a lot of items on your desktop and you make the screen appear larger, then some of those items may not appear on the screen.

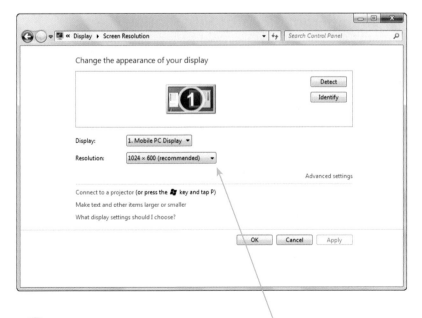

4 Click on the down arrow on the Resolution box which will open the Resolution settings box

...cont'd

5 Use the slider to change the resolution of your netbook screen noting that the slider will show the maximum and the minimum resolutions available to you

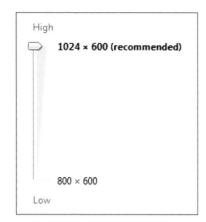

High
1024 × 600 (recommended)

800 × 600
Low

6 Click Apply to see the changes

7 If you are happy click Keep changes or after a few seconds the display will go back to how it was prior to the change

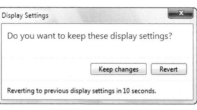

Display Settings

Do you want to keep these display settings?

Keep changes   Revert

Reverting to previous display settings in 10 seconds.

The screen should now look different with everything appearing either larger or smaller, depending on your selection.

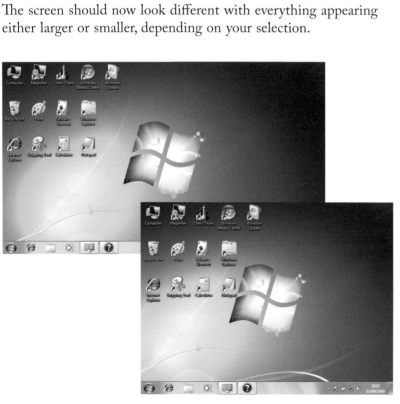

Making it Easier to See

If you are having trouble reading the text on screen or seeing the icons, then you have the option to make them bigger, and thus easier to see. You can do this without the need to change the screen resolution.

1 Click on the Start button

2 Click on Control Panel

3 Click on Appearance and Personalization

Appearance and Personalization
Change the theme
Change desktop background
Adjust screen resolution

4 From the Display menu click on Make text and other items larger or smaller

Display
Make text and other items larger or smaller

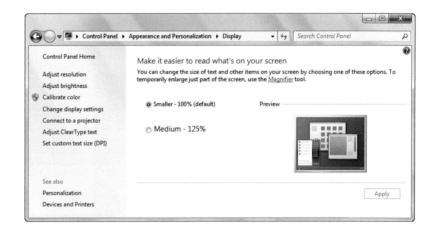

5 Click on the size option you want to choose

6 Click on Apply

7 Either restart your netbook or log off and back on again

⚠ This change will take effect the next time you log on.

Adjusting the Volume

You may want to adjust the volume for the sounds that come from your netbook speakers, either making them louder or quieter depending on the situation. You can also mute them if you don't want sound at all.

1. Click the Start button

2. Click on Control Panel

3. Click on Hardware and Sound

Hardware and Sound
View devices and printers
Add a device
Connect to a projector
Adjust commonly used mobility settings

4. From the Sound menu click on Adjust system volume

Sound
Adjust system volume | Change system sounds | Manage audio devices

5. Use the slider to change either the speaker volume, the system sounds volume, or both

6. If you want to mute or unmute the volume, just click on the speaker at the bottom of the sliders

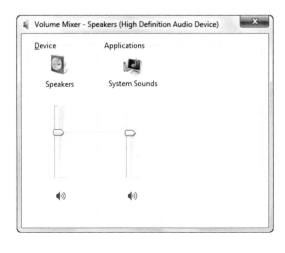

Volume Mixer - Speakers (High Definition Audio Device)

Device   Applications

Speakers   System Sounds

7. Close the window when you are finished

Beware

If you are using your netbook in a public place or on a train or plane, be considerate of others and don't have it too loud, or use headphones.

43

Hot tip

You can actually change the sounds that Windows uses for certain events. See Chapter 5 for how to do this.

Windows Mobility Center

As you have now seen, you can change some of the settings for your netbook through various options accessed via Control Panel. There is also a quicker way for some of those settings to be changed. This is where the Windows Mobility Center comes in. From the Windows Mobility Center you can easily change the most commonly used settings for elements that affect your netbook, such as the sound volume and screen brightness, without having to click through different options per element.

1 Click on the Start button

2 Click on Control Panel

3 Click on the Hardware and Sound link

Hardware and Sound
View devices and printers
Add a device
Connect to a projector
Adjust commonly used mobility settings

4 Click on Windows Mobility Center

Windows Mobility Center
Adjust commonly used mobility settings

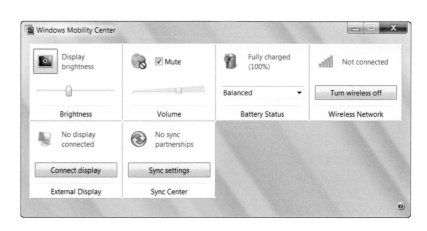

5 Adjust the setting or settings for the various elements

Some of the changes can be made directly from the Windows Mobility Center while others will open up the specific settings page where you can make the changes.

3 Batteries and Power

The battery is probably the single most important part of your netbook. This chapter will explain about the battery, how to get the most out of it and more.

Types of Battery

Don't forget

The amount of use you can get out of a netbook battery will depend on a number of different factors including what you are actually doing with the netbook.

The netbook battery is probably the most important piece of equipment you have with your netbook. The type of battery you use will determine how long you can use the netbook without needing to either recharge the battery, replace the battery or connect the netbook to a power supply. It will also have an effect on the size and weight of the netbook.

There are different types of netbook batteries:

- Three cell batteries – this is probably the most common type of battery in use in netbooks today. They are small, lightweight and provide anywhere up to around four hours of use

- Six cell batteries – these newer batteries provide a significant increase in usage, but the trade-off is the size and weight of the battery. Often a six cell battery will stick out of the netbook and change its overall shape. They can provide anywhere up to around 11 hours of use

- Nine cell batteries – these batteries tend to be manufactured by third parties rather than the netbook manufacturer at the moment. They claim to get even more usage time but again the trade-off is in size and weight

Beware

If you want to get the best battery for your netbook you should consider buying it from the netbook manufacturer.

Don't forget

The size and type of netbook battery available will depend on the specific netbook so have a look at the manufacturer's website to see what is available.

Using the Battery

Anytime you use the netbook without the power being connected, the battery will be used and it will deplete. In fact, even switched off, the battery will slowly deplete, but don't worry, this is normal.

The amount of use you can get out of a fully charged battery will depend on a number of factors, including the type of battery you are using, but the primary factor is what tasks you are performing with the netbook.

Normal everyday tasks such as checking your email or surfing the Internet won't deplete the battery too quickly, however processor intensive tasks or ones that use extra power will. These include:

- Powering external devices via the USB connectors – these devices could include an external DVD drive, mobile broadband modem, wireless mouse and others

- Watching DVDs

- Listening to CDs

- Editing video, music or photographs

- Using wireless

- Using bluetooth

- Having unnecessary programs running all the time

Monitoring Your Battery Usage

So that you can easily tell how much battery power you still have remaining, Windows provides a battery icon on the bottom right hand side of the Taskbar.

If you hover your mouse pointer over the battery icon you will see how much battery power is remaining both in time and as a percentage.

You can do a number of different things in order to both conserve battery power and also to extend the life of the battery.

Beware

If your battery is nearly drained, make sure that you save all your files so that you don't lose anything when the power is completely gone and you won't be able to recover them.

Don't forget

If the battery icon includes a picture of a power cable, this means that the netbook is using mains power.

Hot tip

If you are able, why not use the netbook plugged into the power rather than using the battery? This means that you won't risk losing anything if the battery runs out and it will also charge your battery at the same time.

Power Options

In order to maximise the amount of battery power on your netbook, you can make changes to how your netbook and Windows will use that battery power, which can extend it a lot more than you might think.

To view the options for power management:

1 Click on the Start button

2 Click on the Control Panel button

3 Click on the Hardware and Sound link

4 Click on the Power Options link

Power Options
Change battery settings | Change what the power buttons do |
Require a password when the computer wakes | Change when the computer sleeps |
Adjust screen brightness

Power Plans

Power plans are an easy way for you choose between performance and saving the netbook battery. The main choice is between Balanced and High Performance. If you don't plan on doing anything too processor intensive, then stick with the Balanced plan as this will give you more battery life.

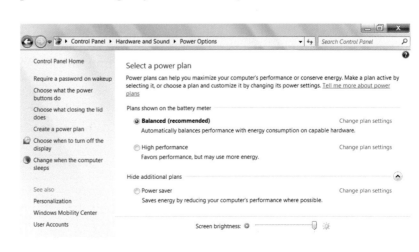

Don't forget

Whatever Power Plan you choose will be used for both battery power and mains power.

Hot tip

You can also change the screen brightness by moving the scroll bar left for dimmer or right for brighter. It's amazing how much battery is used when having the screen on full brightness.

Changing Power Plan Settings

Even though you have selected a power plan, you can still change the elements that make up that plan.

For example, you may want to use the Balanced power plan to increase the battery life on your netbook but you may also want the display brightness to be a little brighter than the plan has set.

These settings also allow you to decide when to dim the display, when to turn off the display and even when to put your netbook to sleep. These are useful if you are going to have your netbook switched on but not use it for a while.

To change the power plan settings:

1 Click on Change plan settings for the power plan you want to change

Change settings for the plan: Balanced

Choose the sleep and display settings that you want your computer to use.

	On battery	Plugged in
Dim the display:	2 minutes	5 minutes
Turn off the display:	5 minutes	10 minutes
Put the computer to sleep:	15 minutes	30 minutes
Adjust plan brightness:		

Change advanced power settings

Restore default settings for this plan

2 Click on the drop down box for each setting and make your selection

3 Use the scroll bar to change the brightness if required

...cont'd

Changing Power Buttons and System Settings

There are some additional settings, called the System Settings available to change that don't specifically affect the battery life but will make it easier for you to put the netbook to sleep, which in turn will probably save you some battery power. You can change what happens when you press the power button on your netbook, the Sleep button and also what happens when you close the lid of your netbook. You are also able to set the use of a password when you wake the netbook up.

Hot tip

If you plan on using Sleep mode, it is a good idea to enable the Require a password option so that only you will have access to your netbook files when it wakes up.

1 On the left hand side of the Power Options window, click on either Choose what the power buttons do, or click on Choose what closing the lid does

Control Panel Home

Require a password on wakeup

Choose what the power buttons do

Choose what closing the lid does

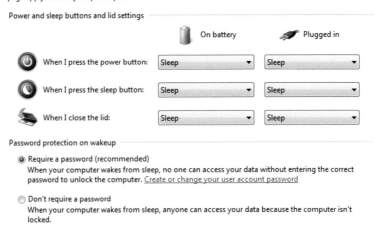

Define power buttons and turn on password protection

Choose the power settings that you want for your computer. The changes you make to the settings on this page apply to all of your power plans.

Power and sleep buttons and lid settings

		On battery	Plugged in
When I press the power button:		Sleep	Sleep
When I press the sleep button:		Sleep	Sleep
When I close the lid:		Sleep	Sleep

Password protection on wakeup

◉ Require a password (recommended)
When your computer wakes from sleep, no one can access your data without entering the correct password to unlock the computer. Create or change your user account password

◯ Don't require a password
When your computer wakes from sleep, anyone can access your data because the computer isn't locked.

Save changes   Cancel

Don't forget

Sleep and hibernate were covered in Chapter 2 so if you need reminding what they are, go back and have a look now.

2 Click on the drop down box for each setting and make your selection

Do nothing
Sleep
Hibernate
Shut down

3 Click on the Save changes button

Creating a Power Plan

Rather than changing one of the existing power plans, you can easily create your own. You can create as many as you want for many different scenarios.

1 On the left hand side of the Power Options window, click on Create a power plan

Create a power plan

2 Select a plan that is closest to the one you want to use

3 Type in a Plan name or leave the default name and click the Next button

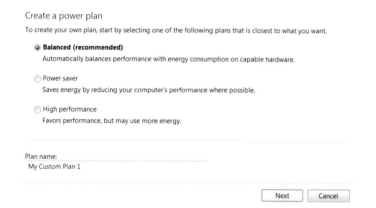

Hot tip

If you are going to create multiple power plans then you should name them something recognizable rather than My Custom Plan.

51

4 Make your selection for each setting and click Create and then select the new plan to use it

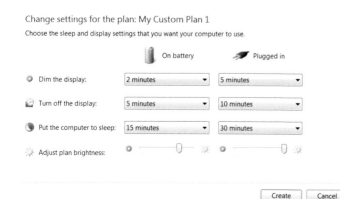

Charging the Battery

The netbook battery is charged using an AC/DC power adaptor that is provided with the netbook. When the power adaptor is connected to the netbook, the battery will charge. If the netbook is switched on at the same time, the battery will still charge but it will charge at a slower rate.

The power adaptor usually comes in two pieces – the power adaptor "brick" which connects to your netbook, and the power cable that connects from the brick to the power supply.

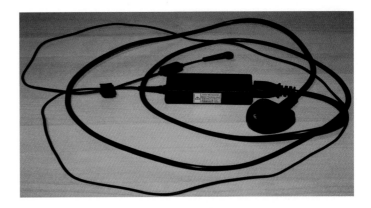

To charge the netbook battery using the power adaptor:

1. Connect the power adaptor to your netbook

2. Plug the power cable into the power supply and switch it on

3. If the netbook is switched on you can see the status of the battery charge by clicking on the battery icon on the bottom right hand side of the taskbar to display the battery meter

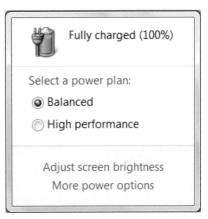

Battery Chargers

Apart from the power adaptor that came with your netbook, there are a number of other battery chargers and power adaptors that you can buy to use with your netbook in order to not only power your netbook when you are on the road but also charge it in locations that you may not have thought about before.

Travel Adaptors

The cheapest and easiest solution to being able to use and charge your netbook battery in a different country is to buy a travel adaptor. These are available in most places and are the size of a large plug and have all the connections for most countries. You just have to select which country you are in and plug in the netbook power adaptor.

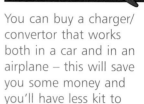

Hot tip

You can buy a charger/convertor that works both in a car and in an airplane – this will save you some money and you'll have less kit to carry around.

Charging in Your Car

Another option is to purchase a car charger – often referred to as a power invertor. This charger connects to your car's battery via the cigarette lighter or power port. It is very small and light and enables you to not only charge your netbook's battery but to also charge other devices that can easily be plugged into it. You can then just leave it in your car ready for you to use next time you need it.

Hot tip

You can buy a charger/convertor that will charge any devices that can be powered by USB, such as an iPod or iPhone at the same time as your netbook.

Charging In-Flight

You can purchase an adaptor that can be used on any aircraft that supports the Empower port (which is most of them). Depending on the type of battery you have in your netbook, and how much power is remaining, you may not need to use it but it can be invaluable on long haul flights.

Don't forget

Check with your airline to make sure that they support the use of netbook chargers and power adaptors.

Removing the Battery

The netbook battery doesn't have to be removed from the netbook very often, but sometimes you may have to. These instances can include:

Hot tip

Unplug the power cable along with any other connected devices before removing the battery as this makes it easier to remove the battery.

- The netbook has frozen and pressing the power button to shut it down doesn't have any effect

- Your battery has run out of power and you want to replace it with a fully charged battery if you have a spare

- You may be asked to remove the battery if you are connecting your netbook to the in-flight power supply on an airplane

To remove the netbook battery:

Hot tip

You might want to place the netbook on something soft that won't scratch it while you are performing the removal process.

1   Ensure the netbook is powered off and the lid is closed, then turn the netbook upside down

2   Locate the battery lock and release, and also the battery

3   Slide the battery lock switch into the unlock position (depending on your netbook, it should show a color to indicate it is unlocked)

4 Slide and hold the battery release switch

5 Take hold of the battery and then slowly and carefully slide out the battery from the netbook

Beware

The battery removal process for your netbook might be slightly different so check the manual that came with yours and never force anything.

6 Place the battery somewhere safe

Re-inserting the Battery

To re-insert the netbook battery do the following:

1 Slide the battery carefully back into the netbook until you hear a click

2 Slide the battery lock switch into the lock position

3 Turn the netbook back around into a usable position

4 Switch on the netbook if required

Hot tip

If you do carry a spare battery with you, ensure that it is charged at all times so that you can easily switch batteries and continue using the netbook without interruption.

Battery Life Tips

It can be quite surprising just how much you can squeeze out of that netbook battery by doing a few simple things. At the end of the day that extra few minutes you have managed to salvage might make all the difference to what you are doing.

Here are some tips for getting the most out of your battery and for dealing with problems that might arise:

- If you don't need to use your wireless connection or your bluetooth connection, switch them off to conserve battery power

- Close down your programs when you have finished using them so that your netbook doesn't need to work harder and use more power

- Try to only charge the battery when it has fully discharged; this is to prolong the life of the battery

- Only connect your USB devices to your netbook when you need to use them

- Run disk defragmentation on your hard drive on a regular basis to ensure your hard drive is as efficient as possible

- Every once in awhile, remove the battery from the netbook and carefully clean the contacts on the battery with a clean cloth

- Don't store your netbook, or any spare batteries, in a hot place or in direct sunlight or in a very cold place

- Turn the brightness down if it is comfortable to do so

- If you are going to shut down the netbook put it into hibernation rather than to sleep as this saves the battery

- Set the power options on your netbook and use them

- If you are doing lots of traveling, consider buying either a spare battery or a specialist battery charger

- If the netbook will not start on battery power, and you know that it is charged, try removing the battery and then putting it back in again

4 Connecting Devices

This chapter will look at a number of different devices that you can use with your netbook and clearly explains how to connect them.

Mice

You might be perfectly happy using the trackpad on your netbook but a lot of people prefer using a mouse as they find it a lot easier.

There are a number of different mice you can buy and use with your netbook – wired mice, wireless mice and even bluetooth mice. The choice is yours, and there are a few things to consider when making your choice:

- How much do you want to spend? Wireless and bluetooth mice are more expensive

- How small do you want the mouse to be?

- Do you want a rechargeable mouse or one that runs on batteries?

- Does your netbook support bluetooth or will you need to get a bluetooth dongle as well?

Wired Mice

Wired USB mice are the cheapest and easiest to connect to your netbook. To connect a wired mouse:

1. Connect the wired mouse to the netbook's USB port

Windows will install the correct drivers, if they are available, and then the mouse is ready to use.

Hot tip

If you want to minimize the amount of kit you are carrying around but still want to have a mouse, look for a small wireless mouse that can easily slip into your bag.

Don't forget

Windows already contains most of the correct drivers for mice, however if it doesn't, you may have to download the driver from the Internet or copy it to your netbook via a USB flash drive or CD.

Wireless Mice

Wireless mice are gaining in popularity as they take up less room in your bag and are less messy to use because of the lack of wires.

Wireless mice come in two separate parts – the wireless mouse itself and also the wireless receiver dongle.

To connect a wireless mouse:

1 Connect the wireless mouse receiver to the USB port on the netbook

2 Install any drivers if requested to do so either from the Internet or from the CD provided with the mouse

3 Pair the wireless mouse with the wireless receiver if required

The mouse is now ready to use.

Bluetooth Mice

Bluetooth mice act in the same way as wireless mice, only they use your netbook's built-in bluetooth capability (if it has one) instead of an additional USB receiver. Bluetooth mice are not as common because not all netbooks have built-in bluetooth and so more people are buying wireless mice instead. If you don't have bluetooth on your netbook you can buy a bluetooth receiver and connect it.

Don't forget

If you are using a wireless or bluetooth mouse remember to recharge the batteries or replace them when they become low.

Hot tip

You may need to pair your wireless mouse to the receiver in order to get it to work. Don't worry, this is simply a case of pressing the connect buttons on both the mouse and the receiver. For more information consult the instructions that came with the mouse.

Beware

Using a wireless or bluetooth mouse will drain your netbook battery faster, so make sure you have enough power or connect to the mains supply.

External Monitors

If you are going to use your netbook for a significant amount of time when you are either at home or in the office, because of the small screen size you might want to consider connecting your netbook to an external monitor, as long as you have one. This will certainly reduce the risk of eye strain and will make it easier for you to view the screen over an extended period.

To connect the netbook to an external monitor:

1 Take the monitor cable and locate the monitor port on the netbook

Don't forget

For more information on screen resolution and settings, go back and look at Chapter 2.

2 Carefully connect the monitor cable to the monitor port on the netbook

Beware

Do not force the monitor cable into the monitor port or you could damage them.

3 You may need to press one of the function keys on your netbook to get the display to appear on your external monitor

Changing Settings for the External Monitor

As your external monitor is larger than your netbook screen you can have a different set of display settings for your monitor, which means you can display a different resolution and screen size from that which is being displayed on your netbook.

To change the settings for your external monitor:

1 Right-click anywhere on the desktop

2 Click on Screen resolution   **Screen resolution**

3 Press the specific monitor function key until your display is shown only on the external monitor

4 In the Display drop down list, select the external monitor

5 In the Resolution drop down list, select the required resolution and then click on OK

CD/DVD Readers and Writers

Because of the small size of a netbook, and also the battery life being extremely important, netbooks don't have a built-in CD or DVD writer. This also makes the netbook lighter, so is certainly considered to be a fair trade-off.

However, if you want to install additional software on your netbook, or listen to music, or watch films or even back up your data to a CD or DVD then you will need an external writer. For the most part these are fairly small and light devices now, and are relatively cheap. They are often powered by the netbook through the USB connector which means that it is one less power supply to carry around.

To connect an external CD/DVD rewriter to your netbook:

1 Connect the USB cable to the CD/DVD rewriter

2 Connect the other ends of the USB cable to the netbook

3 If the CD/DVD rewriter is powered by an external power supply, connect this now

Windows will now show the CD/DVD rewriter as an available drive in Explorer.

Loading CDs and DVDs

Now that you have connected the external CD/DVD rewriter to your netbook it is time to load a CD or DVD:

1   Locate the button on the side of the CD/DVD rewriter

Don't forget

If the CD/DVD rewriter is powered by the USB port on the netbook, it may need to be connected before you press the button to open the tray.

2   Press the button firmly to open the drive tray

3   Insert the CD or DVD carefully into the drive tray

4   Gently close the tray until you hear a click

5   You can now access the contents of the CD or DVD

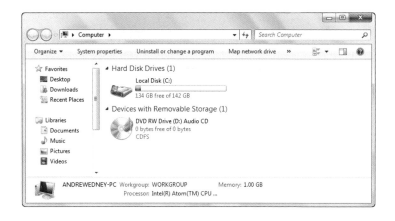

Scanners

Scanners are very useful devices for scanning documents and photographs to your netbook to be used and edited for whatever purpose you may need. There are lots of different types of scanners and they vary in levels of quality and capabilities. For example, you can get scanners that will scan in photograph negatives.

To connect a scanner to your netbook:

1 Connect the USB cable to the scanner

2 Connect the other end of the USB cable to the netbook

 Hot tip

If you don't have a USB pen drive or DVD reader available you could try downloading the scanner drivers from the manufacturer's website.

3 If Windows already has the drivers available for the scanner they will be automatically installed for you and you can start using the scanner immediately

4 If Windows doesn't have the drivers available, or you are asked to install them, follow any on-screen instructions

5 If you want to use the specialist scanner software that came with your scanner you must install it now

6 Start scanning!

Digital Cameras

Most people these days have a digital camera that they like to use when they go on vacation to record events, or at their children's parties, or for many other reasons. The digital photographs are stored on memory cards within the camera, and if you want to access those photographs on your netbook you will need to connect your camera to your netbook and import them.

To connect a digital camera to your netbook:

1 Connect the USB cable to the digital camera – the connector on the camera is often hidden away under a flap on the side of the camera

2 Connect the other ends of the USB cable to the netbook

3 On the digital camera, set the camera mode to playback – you may need to consult your camera manual for information on how to do this

4 Switch on the camera

Hot tip

If your netbook has a digital memory card reader built in then you can just remove the memory card from the camera and put it in the reader.

Beware

Digital cameras can be easily damaged so do not force the flap on the digital camera when connecting the cable.

Hot tip

For information on using Windows to do various things with your photographs, such as importing them, editing them and sharing them on the Internet, see later in the book.

Printers

There will come a time when you will want, or need, to print something from your netbook. This might be a word processing document, a photograph or even an email. To do this you will need to connect a printer to your netbook. Most printers have a number of different ports on them for connection – USB, Parallel and even Ethernet ports for connecting over a network. The most common port is USB and all modern printers have them.

To connect a USB printer to your netbook:

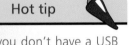

Don't forget

Make sure you have the correct USB cable to connect your netbook to your printer.

1 Connect the USB cable to the printer

2 Connect the other end of the USB cable to the netbook

Hot tip

If you don't have a USB pen drive or DVD reader available you could try downloading the scanner drivers from the manufacturer's website.

3 Switch on the printer

4 If Windows already has the drivers available for the printer they will be automatically installed for you and you can start using the printer immediately

5 If Windows doesn't have the drivers available, or you are asked to install them, follow any on-screen instructions – this may include downloading the drivers via Windows Update

Hot tip

For information on how to connect to a printer connected to a network, including wireless printers, see Chapter 6.

Removable Drives

Removable drives come in all shapes and sizes, and even colors. The two you are likely to come into contact with, and need, are USB pen drives or external hard drives.

USB Pen Drives

USB pen drives are very cheap, small and extremely popular. You may have also heard them called USB sticks, thumb drives, USB drives and so on. They come in a variety of different sizes, and the bigger the capacity, the more expensive the drive.

Beware

A USB pen drive is small and therefore very easy to lose. Take great care with it – you don't want anyone else to have access to your data.

External Hard Drives

External hard drives have a bigger capacity than USB pen drives, which means that they can hold a lot more of your data. They are more expensive than USB pen drives though. And in order to connect them to your netbook you will need a USB cable, which is usually provided with the drive.

Don't forget

You will need a USB cable to connect the external hard drive to your netbook, so don't forget to carry it with you – you can always buy a short cable if you are concerned about space.

1. Connect the external drive to a spare USB port on your netbook

2. The AutoPlay box will be displayed – click Open folder to view files

Other Useful Devices

There are a number of other really useful devices and additions you can get for your netbook in order to make your user experience that much better.

Here are just a few that you should consider:

USB Hub
Depending on the amount of USB ports that your netbook has, you may find that you need more. For example, if your external CD/DVD rewriter needs an additional USB port to power it, then just that device alone will use two ports. USB hubs are small and can increase the number of ports from two additional ports upwards and just use a single USB port on your netbook.

 Don't forget

Any device that connects to your netbook and uses power from the netbook will deplete the battery faster than if you didn't have it connected.

USB Extension Cable
Depending on the location of your USB ports on your netbook, and the type of device that you are connecting, you may find it useful to buy a USB extension cable. This just connects to your netbook and extends the port.

Bluetooth Dongle
If you want to use a bluetooth device with your netbook, such as a printer, and your netbook doesn't have built-in bluetooth then you will need a bluetooth dongle which connects via USB.

5 Exploring Windows 7

This chapter will show you some of the new features of Windows 7 and explains how to get the most out of this new operating system.

The Windows Desktop

The Windows Desktop is the main place where everything is done. From the desktop you can launch programs, shut down your netbook, and do all sorts of other tasks.

The Windows Desktop is broken up into multiple areas:

The Desktop
The desktop is the main screen and any desktop icons that are available are shown on here. You just need to double-click them.

Explorer Windows
Whenever you open a window, such as when you click on a Library, an Explorer window will open and show you the contents.

The Taskbar
Program buttons and other shortcuts can be found on the taskbar.

Tasktray
The tasktray contains icons that can provide you with additional information, such as the Action Center and network information.

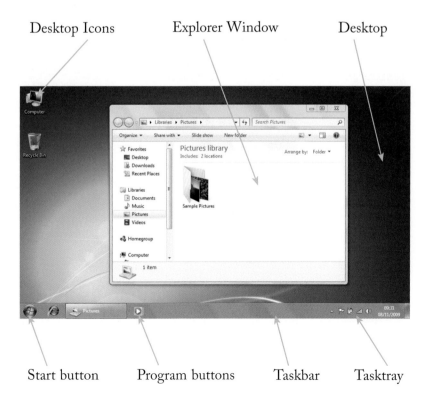

Desktop Icons   Explorer Window   Desktop

Start button   Program buttons   Taskbar   Tasktray

The Taskbar

If you have ever used Windows before, you are probably used to seeing, if not using, the Windows Taskbar.

The taskbar is the bottom area of the screen that on the left hand-side has the Windows Start button and on the right-hand side has the date and time, and in the middle has the launched programs.

Hot tip

If you have used Windows before you will probably notice that the taskbar is a little different than you might be used to – for example, the quick launch toolbar has gone. Don't worry, you will get used to the new way of doing things with Windows 7.

The taskbar shows you what programs you have running and allows you to easily switch between them by just clicking on the required running program.

If you have opened multiple instances of the same program, for example, you have several different web pages open in Internet Explorer, you will see that the Internet Explorer icon now has a couple of extra lines to the right of it – this signifies multiple instances, although it can be quite hard to see sometimes.

If you do have multiple instances open you can easily see what they are without having to open each one. All you need to do is hover your mouse pointer over the program icon and a preview will appear. You can then easily click on whichever instance you want to view, or even close it down.

...cont'd

Hot tip

You can easily rearrange the pinned programs by dragging them to the left or right, or even removing them completely if you don't want them there.

Hot tip

You can also pin any program to the Start Menu using the same process – so instead of it appearing on the Taskbar it will be in the Start menu. You can also have the program appear in both locations if that is what you choose.

Pinned Programs

The Windows 7 taskbar now allows you to pin any program to it so that it sits there ready to be launched. This can save you some time as you will no longer have to click on the Start button and work your way through the list of programs to find what it is that you want to run.

By default, there are three programs already pinned to the taskbar ready to launch:

● Internet Explorer

● Windows Explorer

● Media Player

To pin any other program to the taskbar:

1 Click on the Start button

2 Locate the program that you want to add to the taskbar

3 Right click on the program

Pin to Taskbar
Pin to Start Menu

4 Click Pin to Taskbar

To unpin any program from the taskbar:

1 Right click on the program you want to unpin

2 Click on Unpin this program from taskbar

Jump Lists

Jump lists are a new feature of Windows 7, and provide a very easy and quick way for you to get to files that you have recently used and to access them again.

Instead of finding the program you want, opening it, then finding and opening the file you want to use in that program you can now just click on the jump list for that program and pick the file you want to open.

Jump lists work with any program in the Start menu or on the taskbar.

To use a jump list from an application:

1. Find the program you want to look at the jump list for

2. Right click on the program to see the jump list

3. Click on your selection from the jump list to open it

4. If you use that item frequently, you can pin it to the jump list so that it always appears, regardless of when you last opened it. Just highlight the selection and then click on the pin icon to the right of the selection

Don't forget

If you have used a previous version of Windows, a similar feature was available called Recent Files.

Don't forget

The jump list for any program will only contain the last few opened files, it won't contain everything you have ever opened in that program.

Hot tip

Pinning items to the jump list saves you a lot of time, especially if it is something you want to only open infrequently.

Libraries

Different people store their files in different places on their netbooks – it's a fact. Sometimes this makes it difficult for you to find what you are looking for, especially if you have lots of files and lots of places to store them.

This is where Libraries come in. Libraries is a feature that enables you to find, organize and manage your files easily. A library gathers your files from different locations and displays them in the library for you – which saves you having to search every location for them.

There are four default libraries:

- Documents
- Music
- Pictures
- Videos

74

To view the default Libraries area:

1 Click on the Start button

2 Click on Computer

3 Click on Libraries in the left hand column

You can easily add additional folders to the library which in turn makes it easier for you to view all your files from a single location on your netbook.

To add an additional folder to your library:

1 From the Library, click the New library button

2 Type in a name for the new library – if for some reason you can't enter any text press the F2 key to edit it

3 Double-click on the new library

4 Click on the Include a folder button

5 Locate the folder you want to include in the library and click on the Include folder button

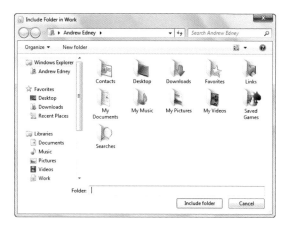

The folder will now be added to the library and will appear along with the four default libraries for you to click on.

Personalizing the Desktop

We all like to have our desktop looking a particular way – maybe it's a favorite background, or colors we prefer. Whatever it is that you want, you can probably make the changes with just a few clicks of the mouse.

To personalize the desktop:

1 Click on the Start button

2 Click on Control Panel

3 Click on Appearance and Personalization

Personalization
Change the theme | Change desktop background | Change window glass colors
Change sound effects | Change screen saver

4 Click on Personalization

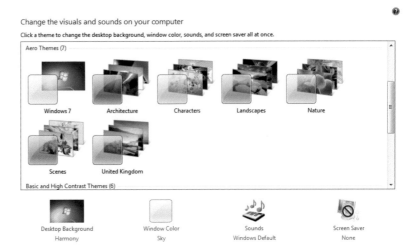

From here you can choose to change a number of features, including the desktop background, the Window color and even the complete Windows theme itself, just with a few clicks.

Changing the Desktop Background

Instead of having the default Windows background, you can use any background that you choose.

To change the desktop background:

1 From the Personalization window, click on the Desktop Background link

Desktop Background
Harmony

2 Scroll through the displayed list of backgrounds and click on one that you like

3 If you want to choose your own desktop background picture that is currently stored in another folder, click on the Browse button

4 Locate the folder containing the picture and click OK

5 Select the picture you want to use by clicking on it

6 Click on the Save changes button

Desktop Gadgets

Gadgets are small programs that run on the Windows desktop and are useful in helping you to be more productive (some of the time). These gadgets include calendars and calculators, amongst many other things. Windows comes with a few gadgets to choose from or you can search on the Internet and download more.

To add a gadget to your desktop:

Beware

Gadgets use valuable system resources so only run the ones you really need to run and if you notice your netbook starting to slow down try closing some of them and see if that makes a difference.

1 Right click on the desktop

2 Click on Gadgets from the list

3 Double click on any gadget that you want to add to your desktop

Hot tip

You can find more gadgets by searching with your favorite search engine – just remember if you are not sure about the source of the gadget you should steer clear of it as you don't want to install a potential security problem.

4 To search the Internet for more gadgets click on the Get more gadgets online link and choose from any that are shown

5 If you want to remove a gadget just hover the mouse over the gadget and click on the X button to close it

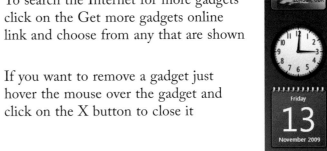

78

A Bigger Mouse Pointer

With the smaller size screen of your netbook, it can sometimes be quite difficult to see the mouse pointer on the screen. If you are having difficulty seeing the mouse pointer, you can make it bigger and even change the pointer itself.

To make changes to the mouse pointer:

1 Click on the Start button and then Control Panel

2 From Devices and Printers, click on Mouse

3 Click on the Pointers tab

4 Click on the Scheme drop down list and choose a new scheme – for example the Windows Aero (extra large) scheme

5 If you are happy with your selection click on the OK button to save it

6 Additional changes can be made by clicking on the Pointer Options tab – including the speed of the mouse movement and also some visibility options

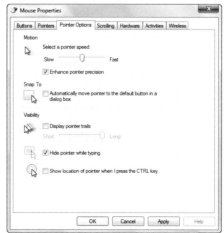

7 Click OK to finish

Don't forget

If you change your mind and want to go back to what you originally had, all you have to do is click on the Use Default button and everything will be back to the way it was before.

The Computer Folder

You may have noticed an icon on your desktop called Computer and also a link on the Start menu with the same name.

This is the Computer folder, and from here you can both see, and access, your netbook's hard drive, and any other attached drives as well, such as USB flash drives or external hard drives.

1 Click on the Start button

2 Click on the Computer button

Apart from being able to then open each drive and view the contents you can also easily see the total hard drive size along with how much space is still available to you for use.

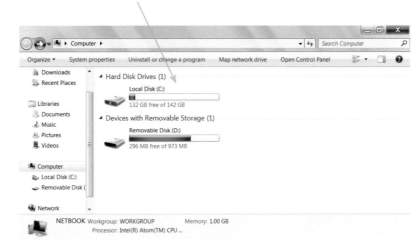

The blue line represents the used space on the hard drive and the remaining free space is shown in white.

Changing the Views

The default view of the hard drives is called the Tiles view. There are a number of different views that you can choose from so that you can change the views to something else if you would prefer.

1 From the Computer folder, right click anywhere on the screen

2 From the new menu, click on View

3 Click on whichever View you would like to select to immediately change the view

View	▶
Sort by	▶
Group by	▶
Refresh	
Paste	
Paste shortcut	
Undo Copy	Ctrl+Z
Add a network location	
Properties	

The different views include:

Icon View

This will change the view to be that of an icon – either small, medium, large or extra large.

Extra large icons
Large icons
Medium icons
Small icons
List
Details
● Tiles
Content
Expand all groups
Collapse all groups

Local Disk (C:)

List View

This will change the view to show the available drives grouped together in a list, including showing the number of devices.

Hard Disk Drives (1)   Devices with Removable Storage (1)

Local Disk (C:)   Removable Disk (D:)

Details View

This will change the view to show the available drives along with information on the size of the drive, its remaining space and whether it is a local drive or a removable drive.

◢ Hard Disk Drives (1)			
Local Disk (C:)	Local Disk	142 GB	132 GB
◢ Devices with Removable Storage (1)			
Removable Disk (D:)	Removable Disk	973 MB	916 MB

Basic Computer Information

Did you know that you can view a summary of basic information related to your netbook? This information includes what version of Windows is running, the name of your netbook and other network information and various pieces of system information such as the type of processor and the amount of memory installed.

1 Click on the Start button

2 Click on Control Panel

System and Security
Review your computer's status
Back up your computer
Find and fix problems

3 Click on the System and Security link

4 Click on the System link

Hot tip

More information about the computer name, domain and workgroup settings can be found later in Chapter 6.

 System
View amount of RAM and processor speed | Check the Windows Experience Index
Allow remote access | See the name of this computer | Device Manager

View basic information about your computer

Windows edition

Windows 7 Home Premium

Copyright © 2009 Microsoft Corporation. All rights reserved.

Get more features with a new edition of Windows 7

System

Rating:	**2.2** Windows Experience Index
Processor:	Intel(R) Atom(TM) CPU N270 @ 1.60GHz 1.60 GHz
Installed memory (RAM):	1.00 GB
System type:	32-bit Operating System
Pen and Touch:	No Pen or Touch Input is available for this Display

Computer name, domain, and workgroup settings

Computer name:	Netbook	Change settings
Full computer name:	Netbook	
Computer description:		
Workgroup:	WORKGROUP	

Windows activation

13 days to activate. Activate Windows now

Product ID: 00359-112-0000007-85749   Change product key

Windows Experience Index

The Windows Experience Index is a tool that assesses key components of your netbook on a scale of 1.0 to 7.9 – the higher the number, the better the performance you will get from the component.

There are five components that are rated:

- Processor
- Memory (RAM)
- Graphics
- Gaming Graphics
- Primary Hard Disk

The base score is actually determined by the lowest of the five scores. You can use this information when buying software that shows the base score needed to run correctly.

To check your netbooks score:

1 From the System page, click on the Windows Experience Index link

2 You can re-run the tests at any time (for example after adding some more memory) by clicking the Re-run the assessment link

Hot tip

Don't worry too much about having a low score on the Gaming Graphics component – after all you probably didn't buy your netbook to play the latest first person shooter!

83

Hot tip

You can print out a more detailed report so that you can have it with you when shopping for software and hardware – just click on the View and print detailed performance and system information link.

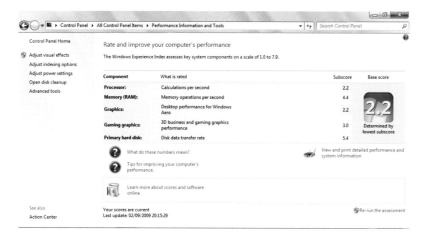

User Accounts

When you start your netbook and go into Windows you log on with a user account. Any changes you make to the desktop, settings, look and feel, etc. are saved for that user account and so it is personal to you.

Adding a User Account

If more than one person uses your netbook, you might want to give them their own user account. To create a new user account:

1 Click on the Start button

2 Click on Control Panel

3 Click on the Add or remove user accounts link

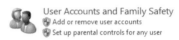

User Accounts and Family Safety
Add or remove user accounts
Set up parental controls for any user

4 Click on the Create a new account link

Choose the account you would like to change

Andrew Edney
Administrator

Guest
Guest account is off

Create a new account

5 Type the new account name into the box

6 Select the type of user account – if this account is not for you then select Standard user and click Create Account

Name the account and choose an account type
This name will appear on the Welcome screen and on the Start menu.

New account name

◉ Standard user
Standard account users can use most software and change system settings that do not affect other users or the security of the computer.

○ Administrator
Administrators have complete access to the computer and can make any desired changes. Based on notification settings, administrators may be asked to provide their password or confirmation before making changes that affect other users.

We recommend that you protect every account with a strong password.

Why is a standard account recommended?

Create Account   Cancel

Making Changes to an Account

You can make a number of changes to any created account, such as changing the name or the picture, creating a password or even deleting the account completely.

To make changes to an account:

1 From the Manage Accounts screen, click on the account that you would like to make changes to

2 Click on the link that represents whatever change you want to make

Make changes to Caroline's account

Change the account name
Create a password
Change the picture
Set up Parental Controls
Change the account type
Delete the account

Manage another account

Caroline
Standard user

Switching Users

If you are logged into Windows and you want to switch user accounts, but you want the current account to remain logged on you can do this. To switch user accounts:

1 From the Shut down list, click on Switch User

2 Click on the user account you want to log in with

3 When you are finished you can either switch back or log off

Andrew Edney
Logged on

Caroline

Windows 7 Home Premium

Date and Time

Having the correct date and time showing on your netbook is very important. If you travel a lot to different time zones, then having the correct time could be the difference between you making an appointment and missing it!

To check the date and time and to change it:

1 Click on the time in the bottom right hand corner of the desktop

Hot tip

Clicking on the date or time will display the calendar for that month. You can also move between months as well.

86

2 Click on the Change date and time settings link

3 Click on the Change date and time button

4 To change the date click on the correct date on the calendar

5 To change the time use the up and down buttons next to the time or type in a new time in the box

6 Click OK

7 To change the time zone click on the Change time zone button and choose from the drop down list and then click OK

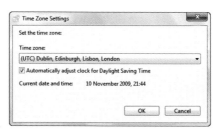

Hot tip

You can have the date and time set for you by clicking on the Internet Time tab – this should already be set automatically for you, so when you connect to the Internet the time will be checked and updated.

87

Adding a Clock

Windows provides a simple way to add another clock, so if you wanted to know the time in another part of the country, or even the world, you can compare the time where you are with the time there. To add another clock:

1 Click on the Additional Clocks tab

2 Check the Show this clock box and select the time zone

3 Add a name for the new clock

4 Click OK

Changing Windows Sounds

If you have ever used any version of Windows before, then you will be familiar with the usual Windows sounds – it's hard not to recognize them! Well you can easily change them, if you want, to something else:

1 Click on the Start button

2 Click on Control Panel

3 Click on Hardware and Sound

4 Click on the Change system sounds link from the Sound menu

5 You can change all the sounds by selecting a new Sound Scheme from the drop down list

6 To listen to each sound, click on one of the Program Events and then click on the Test button

7 To add your own sounds, click on Program Events and then on the Browse button

8 Locate the .WAV file you want to use and click Open

9 Click OK when you are finished

Don't forget

You can use any sound file as long as it is a .WAV file. If you have a sound file saved in another format, such as an MP3, you will need to convert it to .WAV before you can use it.

Search

How often do you want to find something and you just can't remember where you put it? The Search features of Windows have been refined and enhanced to help you even more than before.

To search for something:

1 Click on the Start button

2 Type something you are looking for in the Search programs and files box

Search programs and files	🔎

As you start typing into the Search box, results will be displayed – these results include applications, documents, photos, emails and much more.

3 If what you are searching for is displayed, click on it or click on the See more results link

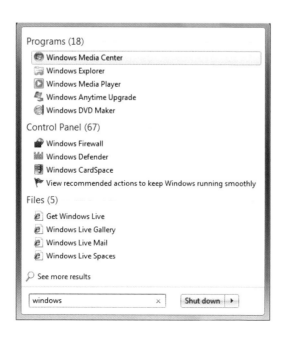

Hot tip

Search can be used to find any files stored on your netbook and it can also be used to find a program – so if you cannot find a program on the Start menu, just start to type the name in the search box and check the results.

Hot tip

As you type into the Search box, the results are refined – so the more you type, the more accurate your search results will be.

Writing CDs and DVDs

There may come a time when you want or need to write some of your files to either a CD or a DVD. You may want to do this for backup purposes to make sure you don't lose your files if anything happens to your netbook, or you might want to give some of your pictures to someone to look at later.

Windows comes with its own built-in CD/DVD writing software so that you won't need to install any additional software.

To write a CD or DVD using Windows:

Don't forget

In order to write a CD or DVD you need to use an external writer connected to your netbook via one of the USB ports.

1. Connect up your external CD/DVD writer to your netbook via a spare USB port

2. Place a blank CD or DVD in the writer

Don't forget

Make sure that you use the correct writable media in your writer – for example, if your writer only supports +R DVDs you cannot use -R DVDs. For more information see the manual that came with your writer.

3. Click the Start button, then Computer, and then double click on the CD/DVD writer icon

4. Type in a name for the disc and select how you want to use the disc – the default option is usually fine – and then click Next

Hot tip

You might prefer to use the software that came with your CD/DVD writer as it will probably provide additional features that the built-in Windows software doesn't provide. But if you just want to write a simple CD or DVD then the Windows software will work just fine.

5. Drag the files you want to write to the disc to the area

6. Click the Burn to disc button

7. Confirm the selections you made and click Next

6 Home Networking

This chapter will explain what a home network is and how to get the most out of it by connecting your netbook and utilizing any available network resources, including file sharing and printers. It will also cover the new Homegroups feature of Windows 7 that makes sharing folders and files easier than ever before.

What is a Home Network?

A home network is simply two or more computers connected together in order to share data and resources, such as an Internet connection or a printer.

If you have a home network and you connect your netbook to it, you can easily share your data between your netbook and any other computer on your network, which saves you from having to use USB hard drives or CD/DVDs to move your data around.

Networking is important if you want to do anything with your netbook either on the Internet or on a home or office network, including connecting to other computers. You can of course quite happily use your netbook "stand-alone" but then you would not benefit from all the added extras that can be gained from being connected either to a network, or to the Internet.

Windows 7 makes connecting to a network, and even sharing files, easier than it has been in the past with previous versions of Windows.

To connect to a wired network is as easy as just plugging in the Ethernet cable into your netbook's network card or port. And as long as the network card and the network you are connected to are functioning, the connection should be made and you can start being a member of the network.

In order to be able to connect your netbook to your home network you will need a few things.

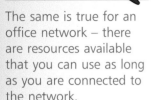

Hot tip

The same is true for an office network – there are resources available that you can use as long as you are connected to the network.

Router/Hub

A hub or router is usually used to connect two or more computers on a network.

Hubs can come in a variety of sizes, one of the most popular being four ports.

Your Internet router may also act as a hub.

The Internet connection will be connected to the router along with a number of network cables.

Hot tip

If you are going to buy a new router or hub, look for one that performs a number of different functions which will mean you can cut down on the amount of kit you need for your network.

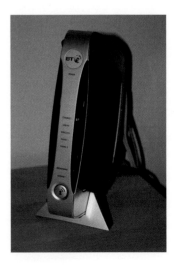

Network Cables

If you have a wired network, you need cabling. This is to connect any devices you might have, for example your netbook to your cable modem. Even if you have a wireless network, there is a good chance you may have something connected via a network cable.

The cheapest and most common form of home network cabling is known as CAT5 cabling.

Local Areas Network (LAN)

A local area network (commonly abbreviated to LAN), is a group of connected computer systems which all share a common communications infrastructure.

In every home or small business network, the networking solution will be LAN-based, allowing the sharing of information in a geographically local area, for example, within a warehouse or office environment.

Internet Connectivity

You will need to have an account set up at your Internet Service Provider (ISP) in order to route traffic from your internal network to the Internet. The ISP will be able to provide the following:

- Physical Internet connectivity, such as through your telephone socket

- A connection device, such as an ADSL modem or dial-up modem depending on your package

- Email accounts

- Website space

- Domain name resolution (access to a DNS server)

- Advice on specific configuration requirements between your own network and the Internet

Hot tip

Wireless networking will be covered in Chapter 8 later in this book.

Hot tip

For more information about going online, take a look at Chapter 7 later in this book.

Connecting to a Network

Connecting your netbook to an existing network is simple and only takes a few moments. Once you have connected to a network you can start using the various network resources, including printers and shared folders.

To connect your netbook to an existing network:

Beware

If the network you are connecting to is not your own, or you are not sure what else is on the network, you should choose the Public Network option.

1   Connect an Ethernet cable from your network to the Ethernet network port on your netbook

2   Select the network location that you are connecting your netbook to (the choices are Home, Work and Public) – if you are using a home network, click on the Home network button

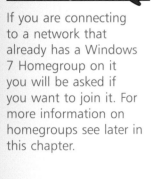

Hot tip

If you are connecting to a network that already has a Windows 7 Homegroup on it you will be asked if you want to join it. For more information on homegroups see later in this chapter.

Network and Sharing Center

Windows has a place you can go to in order to view your network settings, see the status of your network and much more. This place is known as the Network and Sharing Center.

To open the Network and Sharing Center:

1 Click on the Start button

2 Click on Control Panel

3 Click on Network and Internet

Network and Internet
View network status and tasks
Choose homegroup and sharing options

4 Click on Network and Sharing Center

Network and Sharing Center
View network status and tasks │ Connect to a network │ View network computers and devices
Add a wireless device to the network

View your basic network information and set up connections

ANDREWEDNEY-PC   AEHOME   Internet   See full map
(This computer)

View your active networks   Connect or disconnect

AEHOME   Access type: Internet
Home network   HomeGroup: Ready to create
                              Connections: Local Area Connection

Change your networking settings

Set up a new connection or network
Set up a wireless, broadband, dial-up, ad hoc, or VPN connection; or set up a router or access point.

Connect to a network
Connect or reconnect to a wireless, wired, dial-up, or VPN network connection.

Choose homegroup and sharing options
Access files and printers located on other network computers, or change sharing settings.

Troubleshoot problems
Diagnose and repair network problems, or get troubleshooting information.

5 You can click on any of the blue links to get more information or change settings as needed

Don't forget

Make sure that your network equipment is switched on and running and that you have connected your netbook to your network.

Hot tip

This works for either wired or wireless networks.

Beware

Do not make changes to your network settings unless you know what you are doing or what the changes you are making will do – otherwise you might end up disconnecting yourself from the network.

Network Map

When your netbook and other computers are connected to your network, you might find it useful to be able to see a picture of how your network looks.

Windows has a feature called the Network Map which does exactly that – it provides a map of your home or business network.

To view the network map for your network:

1 From the Network and Sharing Center, click on the See full map link

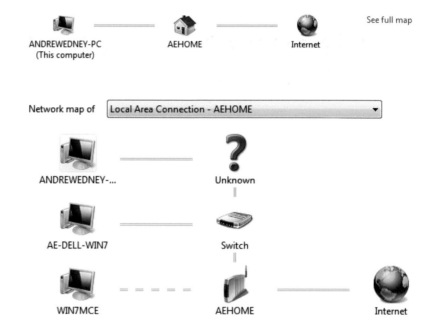

From here you can see all of the computers that are currently connected, where they connect to, and other useful information.

Don't forget

In order for a computer or other device to appear in the network map it needs to be switched on, so make sure all of your computers and devices are on before you open the network map.

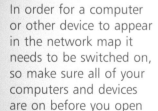

2 Hover over one of the entries in the network map to see additional information such as the IP address and the MAC address

Name: AE-DELL-WIN7
IPv4 Address: 192.168.1.106
IPv6 Address: fe80::97c:6caf:a04f:4c4c
MAC Address: 00-21-9b-1c-0f-43

96

Viewing Network Computers

Sharing files between computers on your network is one of the main benefits of using a network, after all, it removes the need for you to have to use an external drive to move files around.

When your netbook is connected to the network, you can easily see what other computers are available and what they are sharing.

To view computers on your network:

1 From the Network and Internet area, click on View network computers and devices

View network computers and devices

Don't forget

In order for a computer or other device to appear on the network it needs to be switched on, so make sure all of your computers and devices are on before you view the network computers.

2 All of the currently connected computers are displayed

3 Find the computer you want to view the contents of and double click on it – anything that is shared will be displayed

Network Discovery

Sometimes you may not be able to see all of the other computers that are currently connected to your network. There can be a few reasons for this but the most common is that Network Discovery is set to Off which means that you won't see any other computers on your network.

To switch on Network Discovery:

Hot tip

If you are still having problems seeing computers on your network and you have checked that they are all switched on and connected to the network, there is a network troubleshooter you can run to help you.

1 Click on the Start button

2 Click on Control Panel

3 Click on Network and Internet

4 Click on Network and Sharing Center

5 Click on Change advanced sharing settings

> Change advanced sharing settings

6 Click the Turn on network discovery button and also ensure the Turn on file and printer sharing button is selected

Beware

You can also make changes to the Public Network settings from here – just remember that you may not want to share files and have your computer visible on public networks.

Change sharing options for different network profiles

Windows creates a separate network profile for each network you use. You can choose specific options for each profile.

Home or Work (current profile) ⌃

Network discovery

When network discovery is on, this computer can see other network computers and devices and is visible to other network computers. What is network discovery?

○ Turn on network discovery
◉ Turn off network discovery

File and printer sharing

When file and printer sharing is on, files and printers that you have shared from this computer can be accessed by people on the network.

◉ Turn on file and printer sharing
○ Turn off file and printer sharing

7 Click on Save changes

Saving Files to the Network

You can easily save files into your homegroup for sharing with other Windows 7 computers, but what if you want to save files somewhere that doesn't have access to the homegroup or you just want to save them to a specific location?

To save a file to a location on the network:

1. When you are ready to save the file in whatever program you are using, click on the Save As option (or Save if Save As isn't available)

2. Click on the Network button

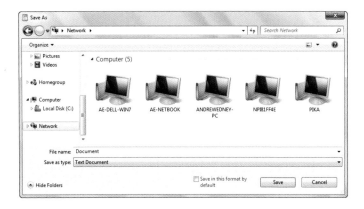

3. Double click on the computer you want to save the file to from the list of available network computers

4. Find the folder you want to save to (remembering that you might not have access to every folder due to security restrictions)

Andrew Edney   Public

5. Name the file and click the Save button

Hot tip

To find out all about homegroups and how to use them, turn over the page now.

Don't forget

Saving files to folders that are shared with your homegroup is the easiest way to share files with other Windows 7 computers, but if you have a previous version of Windows you cannot use homegroups and so you will need to share files in a different way.

Hot tip

If you already have a saved file that you want to copy or move to somewhere on the network you can do this by selecting your file and following the steps from step 2.

Homegroups

Homegroups is one of the best new features of Windows 7. It is designed to make your computers at home work together more easily and efficiently than ever before.

If you have more than one computer at home you can create a homegroup in order to share your pictures, videos, documents, music and even printers with one another. This does away with all the hassle of creating folders, sharing them, assigning permissions and all the various other tasks that go along with what you used to have to do in order to be able to share.

To create a new Homegroup:

1   Click on the Start button and then Documents

2   Click on Homegroup and then on the Create a homegroup button

Share with other home computers running Windows 7

With a homegroup, you can share files and printers with other computers running Windows 7. You can also stream media to devices. The homegroup is protected with a password, and you'll always be able to choose what you share with the group.

Tell me more about homegroups

Create a homegroup

3   Choose what you want to share using the homegroup by checking the boxes and then click the Next button

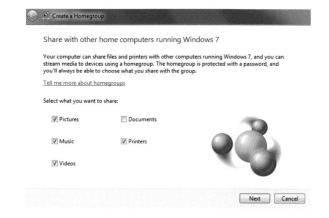

Create a Homegroup

Share with other home computers running Windows 7

Your computer can share files and printers with other computers running Windows 7, and you can stream media to devices using a homegroup. The homegroup is protected with a password, and you'll always be able to choose what you share with the group.

Tell me more about homegroups

Select what you want to share:

☑ Pictures   ☐ Documents

☑ Music   ☑ Printers

☑ Videos

Next   Cancel

4 Write down the password that is generated and click the Finish button

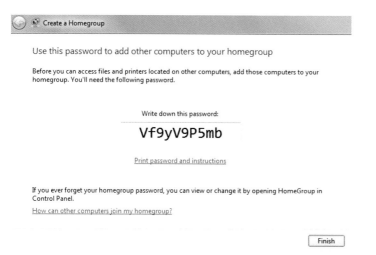

To join an existing Homegroup:

1 Click on the Start button and then Documents

2 Click on Homegroup

3 Click on the Join now button

4 Choose what you want to share and click Next

5 Type in the homegroup password and click Next and then click Finish when you have joined the homegroup

Beware

Keep this password safe because anyone who has access to the password, and your network, can gain access to your homegroup and then your files.

Hot tip

You can print out the Homegroup password along with some additional information by clicking on the Printer password and instructions link.

Hot tip

Don't worry if you do forget the homegroup password – you can easily reset it from a computer that is already part of the homegroup.

Using Homegroups

Now that you have either created a homegroup or joined an existing homegroup, it is time to use it.

To access a homegroup:

1 Click on the Start button and then Documents

2 Click on Homegroup

3 Click on the homegroup you want to access

HomeGroup
Browse available libraries shared by other members of your homegroup.

Andrew Edney (AE-DELL-WIN7)

4 Click on the library you want to access

HomeGroup
Open a library to see homegroup files and arrange them by folder, date, and other properties.

Music Library · Pictures Library · Videos Library

Hot tip

If the folders or files you are looking for are not there, make sure that you have included them in the homegroup.

5 Access the folders and files that you want

Sharing With Homegroups

Sharing a folder or files with a homegroup can be done by simply clicking a few buttons with the mouse.

To share a folder with a homegroup:

1 Locate the folder you want to share and click on it once to select it

2 Click on the Share with button

Share with ▾

3 Click on who you want to share with – in this case it will be Homegroup (Read/Write) because you want to be able to read and write files to the shared folder

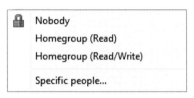

🔒 Nobody

Homegroup (Read)

Homegroup (Read/Write)

Specific people...

4 The folder will now show its state as Shared – you can then unshare it when you are finished

State: 🎗 Shared

5 You can also choose to share with specific users or groups by clicking on the Specific people option and then choosing who and what permission you want to grant

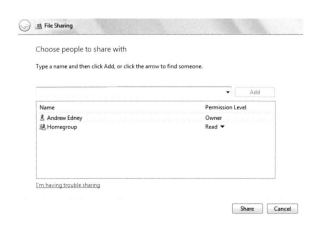

Don't forget

Sharing with the Homegroup (Read/Write) permission means that anyone in the homegroup can update or even delete the files, so if you don't want that to happen choose the Homegroup (Read) permission instead.

Connecting Two Computers

If you don't have a network at home or the office already, you can still share files between your netbook and another computer by just connecting them together with a network cable.

To connect two computers together:

1 Connect an Ethernet cable to your netbook and to the other computer you want to connect with

Don't forget

When connecting your netbook to another computer using an Ethernet cable, you will not have Internet access.

2 After a few moments the netbook and the other computer should start communicating – you can open the Network and Sharing Center to view the status of the connection

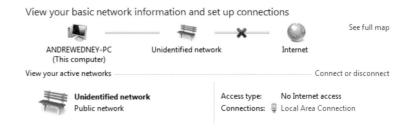

View your basic network information and set up connections

ANDREWEDNEY-PC (This computer) Unidentified network Internet See full map

View your active networks Connect or disconnect

Unidentified network
Public network

Access type: No Internet access
Connections: Local Area Connection

3 You can now view the shared contents of the other computer and start accessing any folders and files

Workgroup Settings

By default, Windows will include your netbook in a workgroup called, unsurprisingly, Workgroup. You can leave it in this group or you can change the name of the group to something more meaningful for you, or you can change it in order to join an existing group that has a different name than Workgroup.

To change the name of the workgroup:

1 Click on the Start button

2 Right click on Computer and then on Properties

3 In the Computer name, domain, and workgroup settings area, click the Change settings link

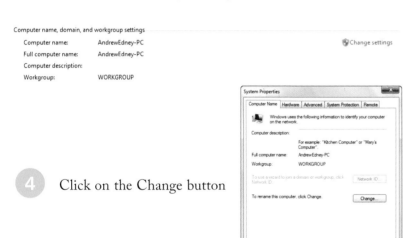

4 Click on the Change button

5 Type in the new name of the workgroup you want to have

6 Click OK

7 Reboot your netbook to finalize the settings

Hot tip

If you want to change the name of your netbook to something different, you can do so from here as well as changing the workgroup name at the same time.

Network Printing

If you have a printer connected to your home or office network, or if you have one connected to another computer on your network and it is shared, then you can print to it from your netbook without having to plug in any wires or cables.

To connect to a network shared printer:

Don't forget

In order to connect to the network printer and configure your netbook to use it, the printer needs to be connected to the network and switched on.

Hot tip

The process for connecting to and using a network printer is the same whether the printer is connected to the network via wires or is wireless, or even if it is a bluetooth enabled printer.

Hot tip

It could take a few minutes to find any printers on your network so be patient and if Windows still cannot find the printer try the Search again button.

1 Click on the Start button

2 Click on Devices and Printers **Devices and Printers**

3 Click on Add a printer **Add a printer**

4 Click on Add a network, wireless or Bluetooth printer

Add Printer

What type of printer do you want to install?

➔ **Add a local printer**
Use this option only if you don't have a USB printer. (Windows automatically installs USB printers when you plug them in.)

➔ **Add a network, wireless or Bluetooth printer**
Make sure that your computer is connected to the network, or that your Bluetooth or wireless printer is turned on.

Next | Cancel

5 Once the list of available printers is displayed, click on the printer you want to connect to

6 Click Next

→ The printer that I want isn't listed

Hot tip

If you have more than one printer it is a good idea to name them something that will be easy for you to remember – for example, if the printer is located in your office, call it Office Printer.

7 Type in a name for the printer, or leave the default setting and click Next

8 If prompted, click the Do no share this printer button and click Next

Hot tip

It is always a good idea to print a test page once you have connected to the printer for the first time – this way you know that it is all working correctly.

9 The printer should then be installed and you have the option to print a test page – then click Finish

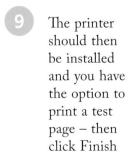

Sharing a Printer

If you have a printer that isn't connected to a network and is only connected to a computer, as long as that computer is connected to the network you can use it as a network printer and print to it from any computer on your network. This is called sharing a printer and is very useful if you do not have the capability to connect the printer to the network, for example, because it only has a USB connector.

To share a printer on your network:

1 Go to the computer that has the printer connected to it

2 Ensure the printer is switched on and connected

3 Go to the Devices and Printers area and right click on the selected printer

4 Click on printer properties and click on the Sharing button

5 Check the Share this printer box and ensure the share name is something recognizable then click OK

7 Going Online

This chapter will show you how to connect to the Internet and use an Internet browser to surf the web and to search.

Connecting to the Internet

Before you are able to browse the Internet you have to connect your netbook to the Internet.

There are a number of things you need to do this:

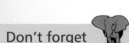
- An Internet Service Provider (ISP) to provide you with the service (this is going to be a service you will pay for)

- A connection method (telephone, cable or wireless)

- Hardware specific to your connection method – for example, if you want to connect via cable, you will need a cable modem or router

The choice of which ISP to use can be varied, although you may only have a small number of options depending on your location. Once you have signed up with an ISP, they will provide you with everything you need to get connected, such as a user name and password, and any other information you might need, including any access numbers, and sometimes hardware such as a cable modem, depending on what you have signed up for.

Often all you need to do is just connect all the equipment together and launch an Internet browser, but if you have to configure the connection yourself you use the Set up a new connection or network wizard:

1 Click on the Start button, then on Control Panel, then on the View network status and tasks link

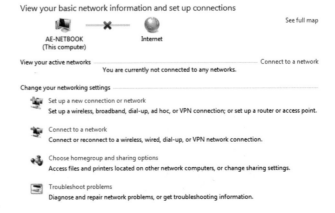

2 Click on the Set up a new connection or network link which will display the various connection options available to you

3 Click on Connect to the Internet and then click Next

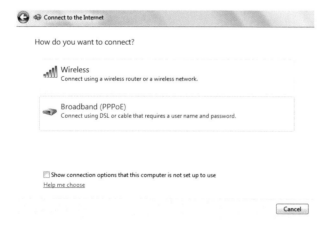

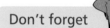

You will only see the connection options that your netbook will support – if you think there should be more, check that all the hardware is working correctly and try again.

4 Click on the option for the way you want to connect to the Internet and follow the rest of the steps in the wizard

5 If you have problems connecting or you need additional help you should contact the ISP

Starting Internet Explorer

Windows comes with a built-in Internet browser called Internet Explorer. You can start Internet Explorer in a number of different ways, depending on your preference:

1 Click on the Internet Explorer icon on the Taskbar

2 Click on Start, All Programs then click Internet Explorer

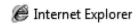 Internet Explorer

The first time you start Internet Explorer you will be prompted to choose your preferred settings:

1 Click on the Next button to begin

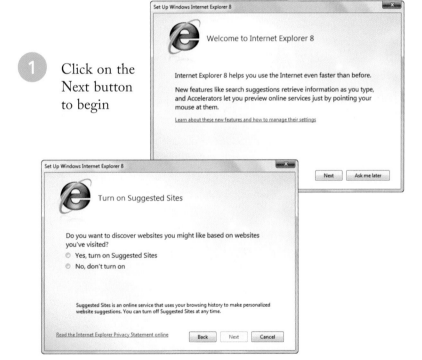

2 Choose whether you want to turn on Suggested Sites or not by clicking the chosen button

3 Click Next to continue

4 Choose either Express Settings (which sets everything up for you quickly) or Custom Settings

5 Click Next to complete the settings selection

There are a number of elements that make up Internet Explorer. The key elements you need to know about to get started quickly are as follows:

Address bar   Command bar   Search box

Status bar   Main window

Surfing the Web

The World Wide Web (or just Web) is a collection of websites from all around the world displaying information on all manner of subjects. Pretty much anything you want to find out about can be found somewhere on the Web.

Each website has a URL (Uniform Resource Locator) which is a unique address, similar to that of your home address (but electronic). To visit a website you need to know the URL. To use Internet Explorer to surf the Web and visit a web page, you need to type in the URL of a website:

Don't forget

You need to have a working connection to the Internet before you can start surfing.

114

Beware

When you type in the URL make sure you type it in correctly as there are a number of websites that will have been registered with similar names that you may not want to visit and can contain material you might find offensive.

1 In the address bar type in the URL, for example http://usingwindowshomeserver.com and press Enter

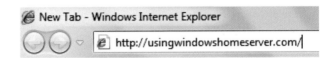

2 If the website is displayed you can start to explore it

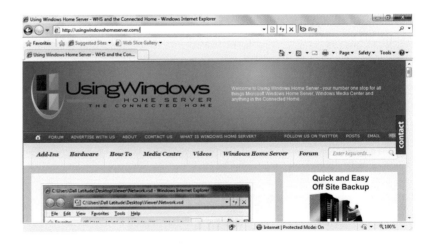

3 You can also go to different pages on the site which are often shown as underlined or different color words by clicking on them

Shockwave and Flash

A number of websites, in fact, a large number of websites, display graphics and animations as part of the page. Often these graphics and animations are provided using either Adobe Shockwave or Adobe Flash, and in some cases, both. In most cases you will need to install both of these products before you can view those websites correctly.

If you visit a website that needs Flash, you will see this message:

This website wants to install the following add-on: 'Adobe Flash Player Installer' from 'Adobe Systems Incorporated'. If you trust the website and the add-on and want to install it, click here... ✕

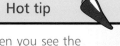
Hot tip

When you see the message you can just click on it instead of typing in the Adobe website URL into Internet Explorer.

To install Adobe Flash and Adobe Shockwave:

1 Open up Internet Explorer and type in the address bar http://www.adobe.com and press enter

2 Click on either the Get Adobe Flash Player box or the Get Adobe Shockwave Player box

3 Click the install options on your chosen installation and then click on the Agree and install now button. Then follow the on-screen prompts to complete the installation

4 Repeat the above steps for the other Adobe product you didn't install

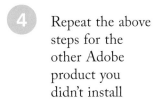

Hot tip

If you don't want to install the Google Toolbar with either Flash or Shockwave, make sure you remove the check in the box before agreeing to the installation.

Searching the Internet

The Internet is a great source of information, providing you know where to look. If you don't have the URL for a site you can perform a search in order to choose from a series of results.

You can search using an Internet search engine web page or you can search using the browser's search box.

Using an Internet Search Engine Web Page

All of the major search engines on the Internet have a web page that you can start your searches from.

Some of the major search engine sites are:

- Google - http://www.google.com
- Bing - http://www.bing.com
- Yahoo! - http://www.yahoo.com

To search the Internet for something:

1 Open your Internet browser and enter the address of the search engine you want to use – for example if you want to use Google enter http://www.google.com and press enter to go to the page

2 Enter the search parameters you want into the search box

3 Click on the Google Search button to begin the search and the results will be displayed for you

4 Scroll through the results and if you see one that you would like to view just click on it

5 After you have looked at the site you can click the Back button to go back to the results and continue looking through them if you still need more

Using the Browser's Search Box

Depending on the Internet browser you are using, there may be a Search box built in, which saves you a little bit of time from having to first visit the search engine website.

To search the Internet for something using the search box:

1 Open your Internet browser and enter the search parameters you want into the search box and press enter to begin the search and display the results

2 Scroll through the results and if you see one that you would like to view just click on it

3 After you have looked at the site you can click the Back button to go back to the results and continue looking through them if you still need more

Hot tip

If you want to open one of the websites shown in the search results but would like to keep the results page as well just right click on the link and choose Open in New Window to open the site in another window.

Beware

Unfortunately there are many websites you probably shouldn't visit for a variety of reasons, for example, they may contain viruses and spyware. If you're unsure whether to click on a link, don't.

Changing Search Provider

By default, Internet Explorer's search function is set to use the Bing search engine, which is Microsoft's search engine. There are a number of different search engines to choose from and it is very easy to change the default to use another one:

Hot tip

You can have as many search providers as you want in Internet Explorer and you can use them at any time by clicking on the down arrow on the search box.

1 Open Internet Explorer and click on the down arrow to the right of the Search box

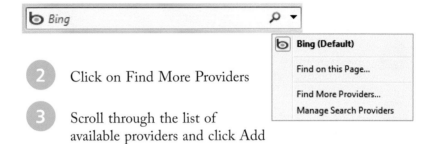

2 Click on Find More Providers

3 Scroll through the list of available providers and click Add to Internet Explorer when you have selected one

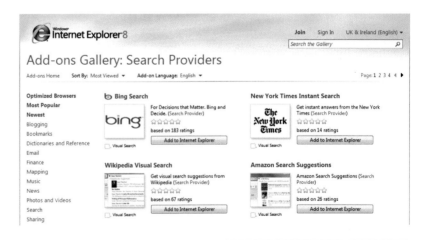

Hot tip

If you do a lot of online shopping at sites like Amazon, you can now add Search Suggestions to search those sites directly from the search box in Internet Explorer without having to visit the site first.

4 Check the Make this my default search provider box

5 Click the Add button

Favorites

If you visit a particular website often, or you find websites that you might want to visit again, rather than having to remember the URL and typing it in again, you can add it as a favorite. Once you have favorites, you just have to click on them to open up the website and continue surfing anytime you want.

To add a website as a favorite:

1 When you are on the site you want to add as a favorite, click the Favorites button

2 Click on the Add to Favorites button

3 Check the name of the favorite and change if required

4 Click Add to add the site to your favorites

To View a Favorite
Once you have added some sites to your favorites list, they are very easy to view whenever you want.

To view a favorite:

1 Click on Favorites

2 Click on the site you want to view from the list

Hot tip

A lot of sites will just say Home as the name – this is not very useful when you want to search for something later so make sure you name your favorite something useful to you.

Hot tip

If you add a lot of favorites they can become a little difficult to search through and find what you are looking for. To make things easier, you can create different folders for topics – such as a folder for anything to do with vacations. Then all you need to do is view the contents of the vacations folder when you want to look for a specific website.

Adding a Different Browser

Windows comes with Internet Explorer 8, but you don't have to use Internet Explorer if you don't want to. You can use any other browser you want, you just have to download and install it first. There are multiple browsers to choose from, with the most popular being Mozilla's Firefox and Google's Chrome browser.

Firefox

Firefox is probably the most popular browser after Internet Explorer. To download and install Firefox:

120

1 Open Internet Explorer (or any browser installed) and type http://www.firefox.com in the address bar

2 Click on the Firefox Free Download button

3 Click Run and follow the on-screen prompts

4 Click Finish to complete the installation and to launch Firefox

5 Follow any on-screen prompts

Google Chrome

Google Chrome is one of the newest browsers available and it is already becoming very popular. To download and install Chrome:

1 Open Internet Explorer (or any browser installed) and type http://www.google.com/chrome in the address bar

2 Click on Download Google Chrome button

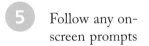

3 Click Accept and install and follow the on-screen prompts

4 Click Start Google Chrome to complete the installation and to launch Chrome

5 Follow any on-screen prompts

Hot tip

If you want one of these browsers to be your default browser that will open automatically whenever you click on an internet link, you can set this to happen in the browser – in fact you may be prompted during installation to set it as the default browser.

121

Don't forget

You can start whichever browser you want by double clicking on the icon on the desktop.

Home Page

Whenever you open Internet Explorer you are taken directly to a web page known as your home page. This home page can be anything and is often set by default to the manufacturer's website.

You can of course change this to anything you want it to be.

The Current Web Page

1. When you are on the page you would like to use as your home page, click on the arrow next to the Home Page icon and then click Add or Change Home Page

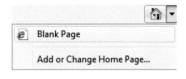

2. Choose the Use this webpage as your only home page button and then click Yes

Choosing a Home Page

1. From Internet Explorer, click Tools, then click on Internet Options

2. On the General tab, type in the URL of the web page you want to use as your home page in the Home Page box

3. If you are already on that web page you can click Use current

4. Click OK

8 Wireless Access

This chapter explains how to make wireless connections and use mobile broadband.

Connecting to a Network

Don't forget

Your netbook will need to have wireless capabilities in order to connect to a wireless network. If for some reason it doesn't then you can buy a wireless dongle to enable it.

Hot tip

The green bars represent the signal strength of the wireless network. The more bars present, the stronger the signal. If you don't have a very strong signal you should try moving closer to the wireless router, if possible.

Beware

If you see more than one available wireless network make sure you connect to the correct one so that you are not using a network you shouldn't be using.

As you have already seen, you can connect to a network by plugging in a network cable. If the network you want to connect your netbook to is wireless enabled you can easily connect to it.

To connect your netbook to a wireless network:

1 Ensure the wireless network you want to connect to is available and broadcasting

2 If your netbook has a switch to enable or disable its wireless capability, ensure it is enabled now

3 The wireless icon on the taskbar will show wireless networks are available

4 Click on the wireless icon in the taskbar to display all available wireless networks

5 Click on the wireless network you want to join and then click Connect

6 If the wireless network you want to connect to has security enabled, you will need to type in the Security key and then click OK

7 If you now visit the Network and Sharing Center you will see your netbook connected to the network and you should be able to access all network resources

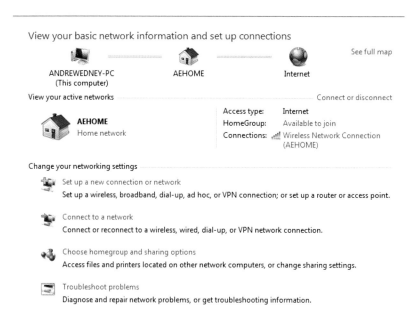

View your basic network information and set up connections

ANDREWEDNEY-PC
(This computer)   AEHOME   Internet   See full map

View your active networks   Connect or disconnect

AEHOME
Home network

Access type:	Internet
HomeGroup:	Available to join
Connections:	Wireless Network Connection (AEHOME)

Change your networking settings

Set up a new connection or network
Set up a wireless, broadband, dial-up, ad hoc, or VPN connection; or set up a router or access point.

Connect to a network
Connect or reconnect to a wireless, wired, dial-up, or VPN network connection.

Choose homegroup and sharing options
Access files and printers located on other network computers, or change sharing settings.

Troubleshoot problems
Diagnose and repair network problems, or get troubleshooting information.

Disconnecting From a Network

When you have finished using a wireless network, or you want to change to another network, you will need to disconnect first.

To disconnect your netbook from a wireless network:

1 Click on the wireless icon on the taskbar

2 Click on the network you are connected to

AEHOME   Connected
                Disconnect

3 Click the Disconnect button

Connecting to the Internet

You can connect your netbook to the Internet in a similar way to connecting your netbook to a wireless network.

To connect your netbook to the Internet:

1 If your netbook has a switch to enable or disable its wireless capability, ensure it is enabled now

2 From the Network and Sharing Center, click on the Set up a new connection or network link

Hot tip

You can use this method of connecting to a wireless network instead of using the previously described method, and this is also the method to use to connect to a wireless broadband router for onward connection to the Internet.

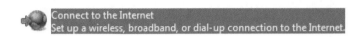

Connect to the Internet
Set up a wireless, broadband, or dial-up connection to the Internet.

3 Click Next

4 Choose the type of network connection you want to use – in this case Wireless

5 Click on the wireless connection you want to connect to

6 Enter any security details you are requested to enter

7 Open Internet Explorer and start surfing the web

Mobile Broadband

Another way of connecting to the Internet with your netbook is by using mobile broadband. You connect a mobile broadband dongle (usually via USB but some netbooks have built-in capabilities that just require a SIM card) to your netbook and then you can connect to the Internet wherever you can get a signal, for example on a train.

The cost of this service will depend on your provider, how much data you want to use and the speed.

To use mobile broadband:

1. Connect the USB mobile broadband dongle to the netbook

2. Launch the mobile broadband connection software

3. If your netbook can find a signal, click the connect button to begin the connection process

4. Do whatever you want to do online

5. Disconnect from mobile broadband when you are finished

Hot tip

There are always good deals to be had from mobile broadband providers so check around before signing up to a deal just in case there is something else better out there for you.

Don't forget

The connection process may differ depending on the software provided by the mobile broadband provider – so read the instructions carefully.

Beware

Make sure that you disconnect when you are finished otherwise you might end up paying for a service you are not using and it can work out very expensive.

Wireless Hotspots

A wireless hotspot is an area that provides wi-fi access for you to connect your netbook to. A lot of places, such as coffee shops and libraries, can provide wireless hotspots. Some of these places, such as Starbucks, will provide free wireless access as long as you are a paying customer. This way you get your coffee and you can surf the web all at the same time.

Some wireless hotspots require you to have an account with the provider – if this is the case you will have to sign up either before you try and connect or when you try and connect.

Connecting to a wireless hotspot is the same process as connecting to a wireless network, although there may be an extra step where you need to enter any account details. When you do connect make sure when you are asked about the network location you choose the Public network to protect your netbook as much as possible.

9 Social Networks

This chapter will show you some of the applications and services you can use to start socially networking online with friends and family.

Instant Messaging

Email is great for communicating with other people, however it can be slow waiting for a response and you don't necessarily know if the person you are emailing is available to respond. Instant messaging is the capability to have a real time conversation with someone on another computer by just typing messages to each other, and you can even have video and voice conversations as well. That way there is no more waiting around for a reply!

There are a number of different instant messaging applications to choose from – it really is about your personal preference. These applications include:

- Windows Live Messenger
- Yahoo! Messenger
- Google Talk

Downloading Windows Live Messenger
To download and install Windows Live Messenger:

1 Open a browser and type http://www.msn.com

2 Click on the Messenger icon

3 Click on the Download button

Hot tip

You can talk to your friends without them having to use the same instant messaging client as you – just be aware that some of the additional functionality may not work – that is to be expected.

Hot tip

Windows Live Messenger can be downloaded separately or can be installed as part of the Windows Live Essentials suite that will give you some other really useful applications.

4 Either click Save and then double click the file to start the installation or click Run to download and start the installation straight away

5 Follow the prompts to install Windows Live Messenger

Using Windows Live Messenger

In order to use Windows Live Messenger, you need to sign in:

1 Type in your user name and password

2 Choose if you want to be seen as available or any other availability option

3 Click the Sign in button

Sign in
Sign in with your Windows Live ID. Don't have one? Sign up.

Example555@hotmail.com ▾

Enter your password

Sign in as: ⦿ Available ▾

☐ Remember me
☐ Remember my password
☐ Sign me in automatically
Forgot your password?

[Sign in]

4 You can now see if you have any contacts online, or if this is your first time using Messenger you can add a contact – you just need to know what their email address is on the instant messaging service they use

5 To start a conversation with a contact, just double click on them from your list and start typing

Don't forget

You will need a Windows Live ID to use Windows Live Messenger – if you don't already have one you will be prompted to create one.

Don't forget

Just because someone is online it doesn't mean they can chat – so try to remember that before sending too many prompts for them to respond.

131

Hot tip

You can group your contacts into various categories to make it easier for you to find them and start conversations with them.

Skype

Did you know that you could use your netbook to make free video and voice calls? All you need to do is install some software on your netbook and create an account on Skype. Skype is the name of the software and the service that enables you to talk to other Skype account holders over the Internet.

To download Skype:

1 Open your Internet browser and in the address bar type in http://www.skype.com and press enter

2 Click on the Get Skype now button

3 Follow the prompts to download Skype

To install Skype:

1 Double click on the SkypeSetup file you just downloaded

2 Click on the I agree – install button

3 Follow the on-screen instructions to complete the installation

Hot tip

Skype provides a number of paid-for services, including a dedicated phone number for people to call so it is worth checking out what they offer as there may be an additional service you might want.

Don't forget

Because the installation downloads software as part of the process you must remain connected to the Internet until the installation is complete.

Hot tip

Some netbooks already have Skype installed ready for you to use so check if you have it on your netbook before you try to download and install it.

SkypeSetup.exe

Creating a Skype Account

Now that you have downloaded and installed Skype, you need to create an account.

To create a new Skype account:

Don't forget

If you already have a Skype account you can just log in with it now.

1 Enter all the details as instructed on the screen including the most important thing which is your Skype name then click Next

2 Complete the details and click Sign in

Hot tip

Your chosen Skype user name may have already been taken so try and choose something that you think is unique but at the same time will enable other people to find you and communicate with you.

Using Skype

Making and receiving video or voice calls is simple once you are signed in. You can add friends to your contacts list and then you can easily see when they are online.

You can easily search for contacts as well so give it a go!

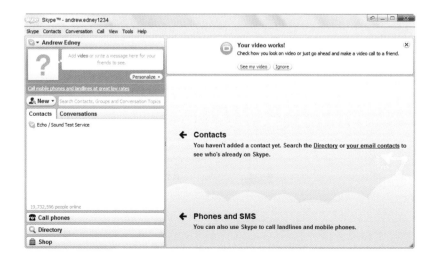

Don't forget

If you are going to use Skype in a public location, consider those people around you and use headphones!

Twitter

Twitter is a fairly new phenomenon sweeping the Internet. Twitter is micro-blogging, which is the sending and reading of small updates from individuals and companies. There are a number of very famous people who tweet (the term given to the posting of an update) and anyone can follow anyone else and see what they are doing. To begin your Twitter journey:

Don't forget

There is no software that needs to be installed on your netbook in order to use Twitter – you just need a web browser.

1 Open your Internet browser and in the address bar type in the URL http://www.twitter.com

2 Click on Sign up now (if you don't already have a Twitter account)

3 Enter all of the requested details on the sign up page

Hot tip

If you use Twitter a lot, there is software that can be used to manage your account and make it easier for you to use if you are following a lot of people. Just do a search in your favorite search engine for Twitter software.

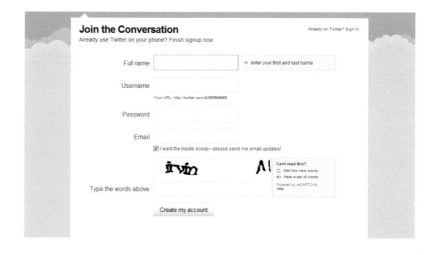

(4) Click on the Create new account button

Signing in to Twitter

Once you have an account, it is easy to sign in to Twitter:

(1) Click on the Sign in button

(2) Type in your user name and your password and click the Sign in button

(3) Type in your tweet and click the Update button

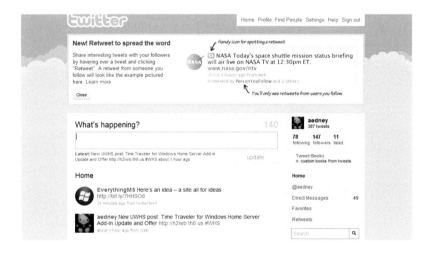

There are plenty of people to follow – just find someone you are interested in and click on the Follow button. Examples include:

- BarackObama - the President of the United States
- stephenfry - a famous British personality
- eddieizzard - a very funny British comedian
- aedney - that's me!

Don't forget

Each tweet can only be 140 characters in length – if you have a lot more to say you should consider starting your own blog.

135

Hot tip

Finding people to follow is as easy as clicking on the Search button and typing their name.

Beware

Just because you think you are following "someone" it doesn't mean they are the real person – there are plenty of people pretending to be famous people on Twitter.

Blogging

There are websites and there are blogs. Blogs are similar to websites but they tend to be specific around something or someone and are usually updated more frequently. Blog is short for weblog – which is just that, a web based log. There are blogs about all sorts of things, in fact, you would probably be hard pressed to not find a blog on something!

Anyone can have a blog – you don't even need your own website to do it as there arc plenty of blog hosting services on the web that are also free – Wordpress (http://www.wordpress.com) is a good example of a very popular service.

Beware

Lots of people blog about all sorts of things, and some people have been fired for blogging about their jobs – so just be careful what you blog about, and remember that once it is on the Internet it is there forever, even if you remove yourself there will still be copies!

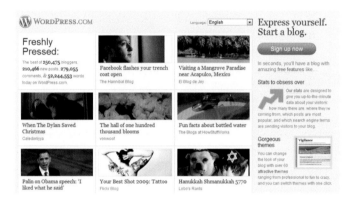

There are many ways to update your blog using various different software applications. One very good application is Windows Live Writer from Microsoft, and best of all it is free. It looks and feels a lot like Word so it's just a case of putting in a few pieces of information about your blog and away you go.

Hot tip

Windows Live Writer can be downloaded from http://www.microsoft.com/downloads or can be installed as part of the Windows Live Essentials suite that will give you some other really useful applications.

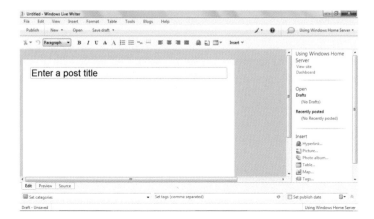

Facebook

Facebook is one of those Internet crazes that you either love or hate. It is a website where you create a profile and then post all about yourself, including what you are doing, where you can share pictures, join groups and so much more.

Other people then become your "friend" which enables them to see what you are doing, share pictures with you, communicate with you by emailing you, leaving you messages on your wall or even talk to you live via instant messaging.

Facebook is free to join:

1 Open a web browser and in the address bar type in http://www.facebook.com

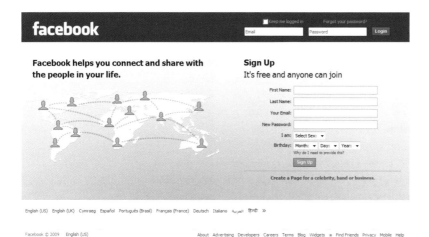

2 Complete the sign up process by entering all the requested information and clicking Sign Up

3 Start using Facebook and post some updates

137

Don't forget

There is no software that needs to be installed on your netbook in order to use Facebook – you just need a web browser.

Beware

Facebook asks for a lot of personal information about you when you first create your account which could be used by someone else to steal your identity. Make sure you set the privacy options on Facebook to protect yourself.

Beware

There are a lot of applications that you can install and run as part of your Facebook profile – most of these actually need access to your account details. Be very careful when agreeing to this as this is an easy way for a hacker to gain access to your personal information.

Webcams

If you want to use video in any of your online social networking, such as video conversations using Instant Messaging or Skype, then you will need to use a webcam. Most netbooks come with a webcam already built in and it can often be found on the top of the lid just above the screen in the center.

If your netbook does not come with a webcam built in you can buy a small webcam that fits onto the top of the screen and connects to your netbook via a USB port.

Most applications that can use a webcam will have their own settings and options that can be configured. These settings and options could include the color settings, brightness, position, zoom and more and will depend more on the webcam capabilities rather than the application.

10 Online Services

This chapter will show you some of the various services that are available online that provide facilities such as email, calendars and file storage and sharing.

Hotmail

Email is probably the most widely used form of electronic communication and just about everyone has an email account, and in a lot of cases, more than one account. Emails don't have to be stored on your netbook or other computer, they can be stored on an email server that sits somewhere on the Internet. That way you can use any internet connected device, such as your netbook, or phone, to connect to the email server and send and receive emails.

There are a number of different free email providers out there, so it is again a case of personal preference.

Hotmail is a very popular email service and is provided by Microsoft. You have the usual email, contacts and calendar functionality you would expect and you get 5 GB of storage for free, which is enough to last a long time.

Sign up For Hotmail

To sign up for a free Hotmail account:

Hot tip

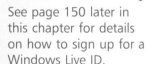

See page 150 later in this chapter for details on how to sign up for a Windows Live ID.

140

1 Open your Internet browser and in the address bar type in http://www.hotmail.com

Windows Live

One Windows Live ID gets you into **Hotmail**, **Messenger**, **Xbox LIVE** — and other places you see

Hotmail	Sign in
Powerful Microsoft technology helps fight spam and improve security.	Windows Live ID:
Get all your e-mail accounts, calendars, and contacts in one place - even if you use other e-mail services.	(example555@hotmail.com)
New! Chat from your inbox, see what's new with friends, and get 5 GB storage that grows when you need it.	Password:
Learn more	Forgot your password?
Don't have a Windows Live ID?	☐ Remember me on this computer (?)
Sign up	☐ Remember my password (?)
More about Windows Live ID	Sign in
Privacy Policy	Use enhanced security

©2009 Microsoft Corporation   About   Privacy   Trademarks   Account | Help Central | Feedback

Hot tip

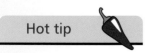

If you already have a Windows Live ID you can sign in straight away.

2 Click on the Sign up button

3 Complete the various steps to create a Windows Live ID and then to sign up to Hotmail

Using Hotmail

Once you have an account, you have to sign in:

1 Type in your Windows Live ID and password and click on the Sign in button

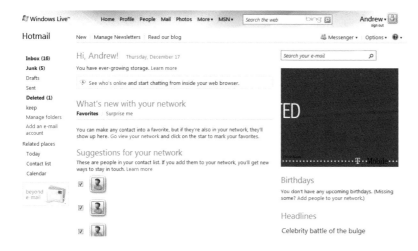

2 To read any emails waiting for you, click on Inbox and then click on the email you want

3 To send a new email, click on the New button

4 Type in the recipient's email address, along with a subject, and then type your message and click Send

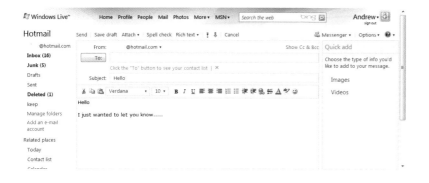

141

Beware

Don't be tempted to check the Remember my password box because this will mean that anyone with access to your netbook can access your Hotmail account without knowing your password.

Hot tip

When you send someone an email you can add them to your contacts list to make it easier to send them an email in the future.

Other Email Providers

There are a number of different free email providers out there, so it is again a case of personal preference. If you don't want to use Hotmail, or if you want another provider as well, two of the most popular are Google Mail and Yahoo! Mail.

Google Mail

Google Mail, or Gmail as it is known, is provided by Google and like Hotmail provides email, contacts and other facilities you would expect to find.

You can sign up for a Gmail account by visiting http://www.google.com/mail

Yahoo! Mail

Yahoo! Mail is provided by Yahoo and offers email, contacts and other facilities you would expect to find and is often used by ISPs to provide email.

You can sign up for a Yahoo account by visiting http://www.yahoo.com/mail

Google Calendar

If you have a busy social or work life you probably use some sort of organizer or calendar. Google offers an online calendar that you can use to keep your schedule on track. You can also share your calendar with friends and family members and also view other people's calendars which makes trying to organize events so much easier than before.

To use Google Calendar:

1 Open your browser and type into the address bar http://www.google.com/calendar

2 Enter your account details and click the Sign in button

3 Use the Google Calendar

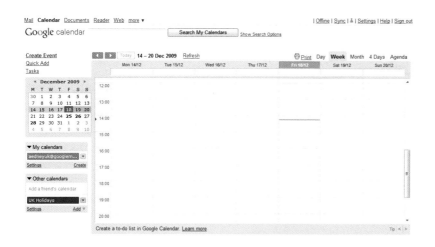

Don't forget

You will need a Google account to sign into Google Calendar. If you haven't already got an account you can easily create one and then use it for other Google online services including Gmail and Google Docs.

Hot tip

You can even sync your calendar so that you can use it on your netbook when you are offline and not connected to the Internet. Take a look at some of the other features that may also be of use to you.

Flickr

Flickr is probably the largest photo sharing site on the Internet. If you want to share any of your pictures with friends, family or anyone who wants to see them then Flickr is the place to go.

Flickr doesn't just enable you to upload your photos and share them, it also provides facilities to edit your photos, remove red-eye, crop and resize and much more.

To start using Flickr:

1. Open a browser and type http://www.flickr.com

144

2. Click on the Sign In link at the top right of the page

3. Enter your Yahoo! ID and password

4. If you don't have a Yahoo! ID click on the Sign up for Yahoo! button and follow the instructions then jump to Step 5 when you have an account

5. Click on the Sign In button

6 Type in a Flickr screen name

flickr

Make a new Flickr account

Choose your new Flickr screen name

7 Click Create a New Account

This can be different from your Yahoo! ID, you can change it later, and spaces are fine.

Note: Your use of the flickr.com site is subject to the Yahoo! Terms of Service and Privacy Policy.

CREATE A NEW ACCOUNT

Upload a Photo to Flickr
To get started straight away and to upload a photo to Flickr:

1 Click the Upload Photos & Video link

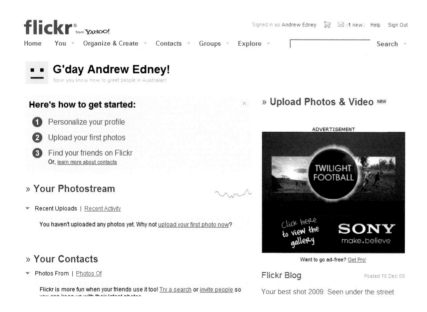

flickr® from YAHOO!

Signed in as Andrew Edney   (1 new) Help Sign Out

Home   You ▾   Organize & Create ▾   Contacts ▾   Groups ▾   Explore ▾   Search ▾

G'day Andrew Edney!
Now you know how to greet people in Australian!

Here's how to get started: **» Upload Photos & Video** NEW

1 Personalize your profile

2 Upload your first photos

3 Find your friends on Flickr
Or, learn more about contacts

ADVERTISEMENT

TWILIGHT FOOTBALL

» Your Photostream

▾ Recent Uploads | Recent Activity

You haven't uploaded any photos yet. Why not upload your first photo now?

Click here to view the gallery

SONY
make.believe

Want to go ad-free? Get Pro!

» Your Contacts

▾ Photos From | Photos Of

Flickr is more fun when your friends use it too! Try a search or invite people so you can keep up with their latest photos.

Flickr Blog   Posted 18 Dec 09

Your best shot 2009: Seen under the street

2 Click on Choose Photos & Videos

3 Select the files to be uploaded

4 Set the privacy level (either public or private)

5 Click on the Upload Photos and Videos button

SkyDrive

SkyDrive is an online storage facility provided by Microsoft that enables you to store up to 25 GB of files for free. You can then access your files from any computer anywhere in the world, all you need is your Windows Live ID.

You can store whatever files you want, and for any reason, simply by uploading them to your storage area. You can share them with friends and family, for example sharing your vacation photos instead of emailing them, or you can just use it as an online backup facility.

To use SkyDrive:

Don't forget

You need a Windows Live ID to use SkyDrive – if you haven't got one yet, now is a good time to sign up for one and you can then use it for any other Microsoft Live service on the Internet.

146

1   Open a browser and type http://skydrive.live.com

Hot tip

Even if you don't plan on using SkyDrive to share your files with anyone it is a good place to hold a backup of your files just in case anything happens to them while you are on the road, or even at home – and it's free!

2   Click on the Sign in link (or Sign up button if you don't yet have a Windows Live ID)

3   Type in your Windows Live ID and password and then click on the Sign in button

4   You can now click on any folder that is visible to view the contents of that folder and you can also see how much space you have available and how much has been used, along with changing any options you want

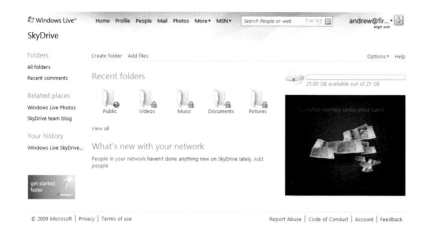

Adding a file to SkyDrive
To add a file to a folder on SkyDrive:

1   Click on Add files   Add files

2   Click on the folder that you want to store the file in or click on New folder to create a new folder

3   Either drag the file to the SkyDrive window or click on the Select files from your computer link and locate the file from there

Add files to Documents
Andrew Edney ▸ SkyDrive ▸ Documents ▸ Add files

Drop files here

Want to browse for files instead? Select files from your computer

Upload   Cancel

4   Add any additional files and then click the Upload button

5   Set any permissions you want to add (other than the default permission which is just sharing with you)

Google Docs

Google Docs is an online facility provided by Google for the creation of, and sharing of, documents, spreadsheets and presentations. There is no software that needs to be installed on your netbook, you just use a web browser.

To access Google Docs:

 Open a web browser and type in http://docs.google.com

Sign in to Google Docs using your Google account and clicking the Sign in button

Start to explore what Google Docs can do for you

Creating a Google Account

As you have seen, in order to use any of Google's Online services, such as Gmail or Google Docs, you need to have a Google account first in order to sign in and use the services.

Creating a Google account is quick and easy:

1 Open a web browser and type into the address bar http://www.google.com/accounts

2 Click on the Create an account now link

3 Complete all the required information

4 Enter the Word verification details

5 Click the I accept – Create my account button

6 Check your email and follow the instructions to complete the creation of your Google account

---

Hot tip

When entering a password for your new Google account, try to make it as difficult as possible for someone to guess.

Beware

Don't re-use an existing password. If it were to be compromised, a hacker would then have access to all of your various accounts.

Creating a Windows Live ID

As you have also seen, in order to use any of the Microsoft Online services, such as Hotmail or SkyDrive, you need to have a Windows Live ID first in order to sign in and use the services.

Creating a Windows Live ID is quick and easy:

1 Open a web browser and type into the address bar http://home.live.com

2 Click on the Sign up button

3 Complete all the required information

4 Choose either an @live account or an @hotmail account

5 Click the I accept button

6 Follow any additional prompts to complete the account creation

11 Music

This chapter will show you all about how to use your netbook to listen to music, copy music to your netbook, buy music and more.

Buying Music and Films

Owning or even renting digital content, such as movies, music and even TV shows is gaining in popularity. It is no longer the domain of just the computer geek, now everyone is doing it.

If you want to buy music or films over the Internet there are a number of ways to do it. One of the most popular ways is the iTunes Store via the iTunes application from Apple. iTunes is an application that can be used not only for buying music or films, but also for copying music, listening to music and synchronizing your digital content with your iPod or iPhone.

Don't forget

iTunes only works with Apple devices like the iPod and the iPhone. If you have a different device you will need to use a different program.

Don't forget

Check the licence for the digital content you are buying to make sure that you can do whatever it is that you want to do with it – for example, some content can only be played back on the device that you used to purchase it on.

152

Beware

There are a lot of illegal music and video websites out there so be very careful when choosing where to buy from as your credit card details may not be safe.

Any site that you buy from will ask you to register and create an account, and will also need your credit card details in order for you to buy from it.

When you have purchased and downloaded your chosen digital content, you will be able to do a number of different things with it including copying it to your iPod or other mobile device, writing it to CD or DVD and more. What you can do will also depend on the licence for that content.

Getting iTunes

If you want to use iTunes for buying music and movies or just as a means to organize and playback your digital music collection, first you need to download and install it. To do that, just:

1 Open an Internet browser, such as Internet Explorer

2 In the address bar, type in http://www.apple.com/itunes and press enter

3 Locate the iTunes box on the screen and click on the Download iTunes button

4 Click on the Download Now button

5 Click on the Save button and choose a location to download the software to

6 When the download is complete, find where you saved the iTunesSetup file and double click it to begin the setup

7 Follow the on-screen instructions to complete the installation

iTunes

iTunes 9
Free for **Mac + PC**

The best way to organize, browse, and play your digital media. Learn more ▶

iTunesSetup

Using iTunes

Now that you have installed iTunes it is time to start it up:

1 Either double-click on the iTunes icon on the desktop or click on the Start button

iTunes

2 Click on All Programs

3 Click on iTunes to open the list, then click on iTunes to launch it

iTunes
About iTunes
iTunes

You can now explore iTunes and learn how to use it.

iTunes has a number of different libraries for ease of use – for example there is a Music library where you can store, delete, update and listen to your music collection.

LIBRARY
Music
Films
TV Programmes
Podcasts
Radio

Connecting Your iPod or iPhone
Connecting either your iPod or your iPhone to your netbook in order to use iTunes is very simple – all you need is a cable that connects the two together.

1 Start up iTunes on your netbook

2 Connect one end of the cable to your netbook via the USB connector

3 Connect the other end of the cable to either the iPod or the iPhone

iTunes should now recognize your device and present you with a view of your stored digital content enabling you to synchronize your content if you want to.

Don't forget

Your iPod or your iPhone will receive a battery charge when it is connected to your netbook – but remember that power comes from your netbook battery.

You can see on the left hand column all of the content of your device, sorted by type – for example by Music, Films, etc.

The main part of the screen shows a summary of your device, including its name, capacity and version number. You can also choose settings for each type of content.

The lower part of the screen shows information on the capacity of the device – in my case I don't have much free space available.

Copying Music to Your iPod or iPhone

There are a few different ways to copy music, or any other digital content, to your device from iTunes. You can choose to synchronize all your libraries to the device or you can be more selective by simply dragging the content you want from the library onto the device.

Removing Your iPod or iPhone

In order to ensure that you don't corrupt any files on your device, you need to make sure you remove it correctly:

1. Right-click on the name of your iPod or iPhone

2. Click on Eject

3. Disconnect your iPod or iPhone

Beware

The Restore button will perform a factory reset on your device which will mean all the content stored on it will be erased – so ensure you have copies of everything before using this option.

155

Hot tip

iTunes will check with Apple to see if there are any updates for your connected device. If there are updates available it would be a good idea to connect via your home network as these updates are often quite large.

Adding Music to iTunes

There are a number of different ways that you can add music, or any other digital content, to iTunes.

If you already have some music stored on your netbook, you can add it to your iTunes music library:

 Click on File

 Click on Add Folder to Library

Add File to Library...	Ctrl+O
Add Folder to Library...	
Library	▶

Locate the folder of music on your netbook and click once on the folder to select it

Click on Select Folder to start adding the music

The music will then be imported into your music library.

Afterglow
Sarah McLachlan

Afterglow Live
Sarah McLachlan

Ripping CDs Using iTunes

Now that you have iTunes installed and working, and you have added existing music to your iTunes library, it is time to start adding music directly from CDs. This process is called ripping – basically you are ripping the songs from the CD to your netbook.

To rip a CD to your iTunes library:

1 Connect the external USB CD or DVD drive to the netbook

2 Insert the CD you want to rip into the drive – if you are connected to the Internet, iTunes will attempt to identify the CD

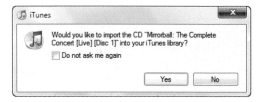

3 If you want to rip the entire album, click Yes

4 If you only want a particular song, or some of the songs, click No when asked if you want to import the CD

	Name	Time	Artist	Album	Genre
1	Building A Mystery	4:23	Sarah McLachlan	Mirrorball: The Complete Concert [Live] [Disc 1]	Pop
2	Plenty	3:19	Sarah McLachlan	Mirrorball: The Complete Concert [Live] [Disc 1]	Pop
3	Hold On	5:10	Sarah McLachlan	Mirrorball: The Complete Concert [Live] [Disc 1]	Pop
4	Good Enough	6:18	Sarah McLachlan	Mirrorball: The Complete Concert [Live] [Disc 1]	Pop
5	Do What You Have To Do	4:14	Sarah McLachlan	Mirrorball: The Complete Concert [Live] [Disc 1]	Pop
6	Witness	4:50	Sarah McLachlan	Mirrorball: The Complete Concert [Live] [Disc 1]	Pop
7	Wait	5:44	Sarah McLachlan	Mirrorball: The Complete Concert [Live] [Disc 1]	Pop
8	I Will Remember You	3:37	Sarah McLachlan	Mirrorball: The Complete Concert [Live] [Disc 1]	Pop
9	Ice	5:41	Sarah McLachlan	Mirrorball: The Complete Concert [Live] [Disc 1]	Pop
10	I Love You	5:45	Sarah McLachlan	Mirrorball: The Complete Concert [Live] [Disc 1]	Pop
11	I Will Not Forget You	5:45	Sarah McLachlan	Mirrorball: The Complete Concert [Live] [Disc 1]	Pop

5 Ensure that each song you want has a check by it and then click the Import CD button

6 When the CD ripping has finished, eject the CD

Don't forget

Because you will need to use an external CD or DVD drive in order to rip your CDs to iTunes, the battery power will go down quicker than normal so you might want to connect the power cable.

Don't forget

Only rip CDs that you own – do not borrow CDs from friends and rip them to iTunes as this is against the law.

157

Don't forget

The process of ripping CDs to your iTunes library via your external USB drive can be a slow process – so be patient!

Podcasts

Podcasts are radio and TV style programmes that you can download from the Internet and listen to on your netbook, or on a mobile device such as an iPod or iPhone. Best of all, most podcasts are free and there are literally thousands and thousands of podcasts on all different topics, so there is bound to be something of interest to you.

To use iTunes to search for and download podcasts:

 1 Click on the iTunes Store link

2 Click on Podcasts at the top of the page

3 Search for and locate a podcast you might be interested in

4 Click on the Subscribe button

The latest episode of the podcast will now be downloaded and stored in your library.

Global News
1 Episode

5 Click on the Podcasts library and find your podcast then click on the Play button

---

Music on Your Netbook

If you already have music on another computer, or if someone has given you a CD of ripped music, or even music on a USB drive and you would like to have it on your netbook, then it is a simple process to copy it over:

Hot tip

You can use this same process for any digital content, such as music, videos and photos.

1 Take the CD, USB stick, external drive, or whatever source of ripped music you have and connect it to your netbook

2 Open the drive and select the music you want to copy

3 Right-click and then click on Copy

4 Click on the Start Button

5 Click on the Music button

6 Right-click and then click on New and select Folder

7 Type in a name for the new folder

8 Double-click on the new folder

9 Right-click and then click on Paste to copy the music into the folder

Music library
Includes: 2 locations

iTunes

Sample Music   Sarah McLachlan

Media Player

Windows has some built-in software to play music and videos called Windows Media Player. Media Player also allows you to organize your digital content, buy music and videos, burn CDs of your favorite songs and even stream music from the Internet.

Media Player supports all the popular formats such as MP3 and AVI files, and is extensible, which means that you can add support for other file types by installing what are known as codecs.

Starting Media Player
To start Media Player, you can do the following:

1 Either click on the Media Player icon in the Task Bar or

2 Click the Start Button

3 Click on All Programs Windows Media Player

4 Click on Windows Media Player

The very first time that you start Media Player on your netbook, you will be asked to make a choice about which settings you want Media Player to use.

5 Make your selection and press enter

The recommended settings option is the quickest and easiest one to go for as Windows will configure everything for you. If you want to make those choices yourself just select the custom settings option instead and work through each option.

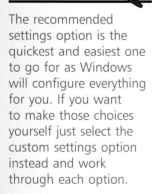

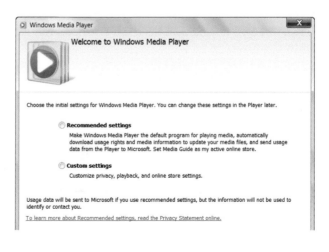

The first screen you are likely to see is the music library. Here you will see any music that is currently stored in the Music folder on your netbook.

Playing Music or Videos With Media Player

Playing your music or videos is simply a case of selecting what you want to play and double-clicking on it.

When you are playing a song or collection of songs, you can pause the song, skip to the next song, change the volume – basically everything you would expect to be able to do.

There are also a number of different views you can have while listening to songs or watching videos – these views include a full screen view and also a mini view.

The mini view is very useful if you want to watch something at the same time as doing something else on the netbook.

Internet Radio

You can listen to your favorite radio stations, or find some new favorites all from your netbook – all you need is an Internet connection.

1. Open up Windows Media Player

2. Click the Media Guide button

3. Click on Internet Radio

You will be presented with a list of genres including Classic Rock and Top 40, there will also be some editor's picks to choose from, but of course you can easily search for something else.

4. Find a radio station you want to listen to and click on the Listen button or Visit for more information

Ripping CDs – Media Player

Ripping CDs to your Media Player music library is very similar to ripping CDs to your iTunes library – the biggest difference between the two programs is that iTunes has to be downloaded and installed where as Media Player is built into Windows.

To rip a CD to your Media Player library:

1 Connect the external USB CD or DVD drive to the netbook

2 Insert the CD you want to rip into the drive – if you are connected to the Internet, Media Player will attempt to identify the CD

Don't forget

Only rip CDs that you own – do not borrow CDs from friends and rip them to Media Player as this is against the law.

163

3 Ensure that each song you want to rip has a check by it and then click the Rip CD button

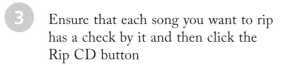

4 Select whether to use copy protection or not and then click OK to start ripping

Don't forget

The process of ripping CDs to your Media Player library via your external USB drive can be a slow process – so be patient!

5 When the CD ripping has finished, eject the CD

Media Player Playlists

If you start to store a lot of music on your netbook, you might want to consider setting up some playlists within Media Player. Playlists are a great way to group together songs that you like listening to or which have a theme – for example, you might want to create a playlist of songs for when you are working out and another for when you just want to relax and listen to music. Windows Media Player has two different types of playlists – regular playlists and auto playlists.

Regular Playlists

A regular playlist is a list of songs that you create for yourself.

To create a regular playlist:

1 Click on the Playlists button

2 If this is your first playlist, click on the Click here link in the center of the screen

3 Type in a name for your playlist and press enter

4 Click on either Artist, Album or Genre from your music library list to start selecting your music to add to the playlist

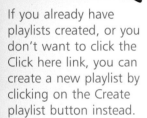

Hot tip

Playlists don't just have to contain music, they can contain pictures and videos as well.

Hot tip

If you already have playlists created, or you don't want to click the Click here link, you can create a new playlist by clicking on the Create playlist button instead.

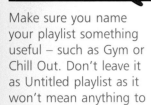

Hot tip

Make sure you name your playlist something useful – such as Gym or Chill Out. Don't leave it as Untitled playlist as it won't mean anything to you later.

5 Left-click on the song you want to add to your playlist and drag it over to the playlist then let go

6 Repeat step 5 for all the songs you want to add to your playlist

> **Hot tip**
>
> You can rearrange the order of any of the songs in the playlist just by dragging and dropping them into the order that you want to listen to.

7 To listen to the playlist, or any playlist, just click on it and then click on the play button

Auto Playlists

Auto playlists are created for you and are automatically changed according to whatever criteria you have selected. For example, you could set criteria so that every time you add a song to your library by your favorite artist it would automatically be added to that playlist for you.

To create an auto playlist:

> **Hot tip**
>
> Both regular playlists and auto playlists can be written to CD in order to create your own music CD that can be played on a normal CD player.

1 Click on the Playlists button

2 Click on the down arrow to the right of the Create playlist button

3 Click on Create auto playlist

165

...cont'd

Hot tip

Make sure you name your auto playlist something useful – such as Gym or Chill Out. Don't leave it as Untitled Auto Playlist as that won't mean anything to you later when you can't remember what it is.

Don't forget

Auto playlists are updated all the time, depending on whatever criteria you selected.

Hot tip

You can convert an auto playlist into a regular playlist by right-clicking the selected auto playlist and clicking Add to, and then clicking Playlist.

4 Type in a name for the auto playlist

5 Click on the green plus symbol under Music in my library and make a selection – for example select Album Artist if you want to include particular artists

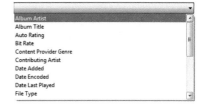

6 Click on the underlined options to make your specific selections

▽ Album artist Contains [click to set]

7 Make any other selections by clicking on the remaining green plus symbols

8 Click OK to finish

Windows Media Player will now search through your libraries against the criteria you selected and will create your auto playlist.

12 Pictures and Photos

This chapter will show you how to import photos from your digital camera to your netbook and how to view, print, email and manage your pictures.

Pictures Library

Windows 7 has a number of libraries, which as you recall are just locations where you store your files. There is a library called Pictures which includes a folder called My Pictures which is the default location for storing your pictures and photographs.

To access your Pictures library:

1 Click on the Start button

2 From the right hand side menu, click on Pictures

You can then see whatever pictures you have stored there.

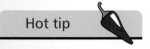

Hot tip

For more information on Windows 7 Libraries, go back to Chapter 5.

168

Hot tip

You can view your pictures in whatever way you want – for example as thumbnail images or as names. Obviously thumbnail images make it easier to see what they are without having to open each one in turn.

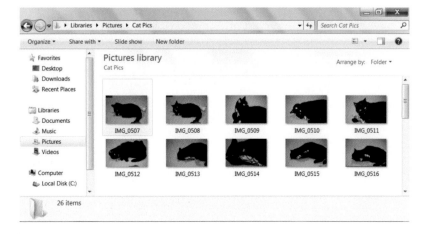

Slide Shows and Views

Now that you have pictures stored in your Pictures library, one of the nice features of Windows 7 is the ability to view those pictures in a full screen slide show.

A slide show will just display each of your photos in turn for a few moments and then move on to the next photo and will continuing going on until you stop it. This can be quite relaxing to watch and also it makes the process of viewing pictures on your netbook easier, especially if you want to show other people the pictures you have stored.

To start a slide show from your Pictures library:

1 Choose the folder you want to view the pictures from in a slide show

2 Click on the Slide show button

3 If you click the right mouse button you will see a number of options for the slide show, including pausing the slide show, going to the next slide or back a slide and even the slide show speed

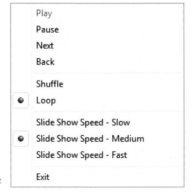

| Play |
| Pause |
| Next |
| Back |
| Shuffle |
| ◉ Loop |
| Slide Show Speed - Slow |
| ◉ Slide Show Speed - Medium |
| Slide Show Speed - Fast |
| Exit |

4 When you want to end the slide show press any key

Views

You can change the views in the Pictures library to show the pictures by folder, month, day, rating, tag or other properties.

Arrange by: Folder ▾

| ◉ Folder |
| Month |
| Day |
| Rating |
| Tag |

1 Click on the Arrange by list

2 Click on the arrangement you want

Hot tip

You can speed up the movement between pictures by clicking the mouse button

Hot tip

You can stop the slide show at any time by pressing any key on the keyboard.

169

Don't forget

Arranging the views by Tag will only work if you have entered tag information for your pictures.

Hot tip

If you are going to buy a USB media reader you should look for one that supports multiple card formats so that you can read any available memory card. This will mean that you won't need to buy another one if you change cameras.

Beware

Never force the digital memory card into the reader – if it doesn't appear to fit check that you are trying to insert it the correct way and that the reader is actually designed for that type of memory card.

Hot tip

Always copy the photographs to your netbook before you do anything with them – that way if you do something by mistake you always have them on the memory card to copy over again.

Importing Pictures

If you have a digital camera, or have been given a digital camera memory card with some digital photographs on then you will want to import them onto your netbook for any number of reasons including viewing them, editing them and printing them.

The three easiest ways to get them onto your netbook are by connecting your camera to your netbook via USB (if your camera supports this), plugging in the memory card directly into your netbook (if you have a media reader on your netbook) or by connecting a USB media reader to your netbook.

USB Media Readers

USB media readers have been around for a number of years and are a cheap and easy way of reading digital camera memory cards. They come in a variety of different sizes and media card types and simply connect to your netbook via a spare USB port; you then insert the memory card into the reader.

Built-in Media Readers

If your netbook already has a built-in media card reader then it is just a simple case of locating the reader and then inserting the memory card into the reader and accessing the photographs.

Windows will treat the memory card as an additional external drive and so you can just open the drive and do whatever you want to do with the photographs.

Connecting Your Camera Directly

The third method is to connect your digital camera directly to your netbook via a USB connector and cable. When you connect the camera directly to the netbook Windows will give you the option of importing the photographs and also provide optional settings.

1 Connect the USB cable to both the camera and netbook

2 Switch on the camera and set it to playback if such an option exists on the camera

3 The AutoPlay menu should appear giving you a number of options including opening the device to view the pictures and also the option to Import Pictures and Videos – which is the option you should click on

4 Windows will now locate all your available pictures and videos on the camera. You can either wait for this to happen or click on the Import settings link to change the import settings

5 You can now add an optional tag to the pictures – such as Vacation 2009

171

...cont'd

6 You can now click the Import button and any pictures and videos will be copied to your netbook to the My Pictures library in a new folder with today's date on them

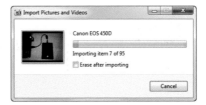

7 If you wanted to change the default import settings then just click on the Import settings link before clicking on the Import now button

8 Make any changes that you want – for example you might want to change the location of imported images and videos from the My Pictures library

9 Click OK and then go back to either step 5 or step 6 and continue the importing process

Add Folders to the Library

The Pictures library actually consists of a location that watches folders on your netbook and includes them for easy access and viewing. If you had a folder stored in another location, for example on your desktop, you could add this folder to be watched and included by the Pictures library so that whenever you clicked on the Pictures library it would be displayed, without the need to copy or move the folder there.

To add a folder to be included in the Pictures library:

1 From the Pictures library, click the locations link

Pictures library
Includes: 2 locations

2 Click on the Add button

3 Locate the folder that you want to include in the Pictures library and click on the Include folder button

Include folder

4 Click OK and you will see the images contained in that folder displayed within the Pictures Library

Hot tip

If you have lots of pictures stored in folders in other locations you might want to consider moving those folders directly into the My Pictures folder otherwise the pictures will be individually displayed instead of firstly having the folder displayed.

173

Hot tip

You can easily remove them from your library by selecting them and clicking on the Remove button – this doesn't delete the pictures, it only stops them being displayed within the Pictures library.

Windows Photo Viewer

Windows 7 has a built-in application called Photo Viewer that enables you to view your pictures and print them as well.

To open a picture in Photo Viewer:

1 Locate the picture that you want to view from your Picture library (or wherever it is stored) and double-click it to open it in Photo Viewer

Now that the picture is displayed, you can do a number of different things, depending on what button you click from the menu bar below the picture:

Magnify   Slide Show   Rotate the image

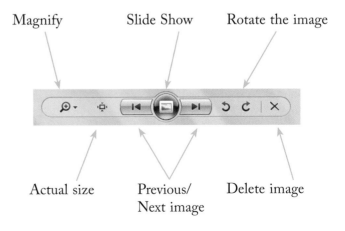

Actual size   Previous/ Next image   Delete image

Emailing Pictures

When you are looking through your pictures you might decide that you want to send one or more of them to people you know via email. If you want to email a picture to someone there is an easy way to do it from within either the Pictures library or from the Window Photo Viewer. This email function also includes the ability to compress the attachments to make them smaller and quicker to send, especially if you have a slow Internet connection.

To email a picture:

1 Open the picture you want to email in Windows Photo Viewer

2 Click on the Email button   E-mail

3 In the Attach Files box decide the picture size that you want to use by clicking on the down arrow

Smaller: 640 x 480
Small: 800 x 600
Medium: 1024 x 768
Large: 1280 x 1024
Original Size

4 Click on the picture size you want

5 Click the Attach button to start a new email message with the picture attached in the size selected

6 Write your email and then send it

Don't forget

In order to be able to email pictures directly from the Pictures Library or from Windows Photo Viewer you will need to have an email program, such as Microsoft Outlook, installed on your netbook.

Hot tip

You can still use another email application or webmail application to send your pictures, you just won't be able to benefit from the compression tools within the Pictures library or Windows Photo Viewer.

Hot tip

For other ways of sharing your pictures take a look at Flickr mentioned in the previous chapter.

Printing Pictures

When you are looking at your pictures, you may decide that you want to print some. You can print a single picture, multiple pictures on a single page or even a contact sheet.

To print a picture from Photo Viewer:

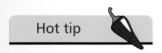

Hot tip

You can also press CTRL and P on the keyboard to start the print process.

1 When you are viewing your pictures and you come to one or more that you want to print, click on the Print drop down box

2 Click on Print

🖨	Print...	Ctrl+P
🌐	Order prints...	

3 Ensure the correct printer is selected, along with any other settings you want to change, including the quality and paper type and what you want to print

Hot tip

For the best printing results, always ensure you have selected Photo or Advanced Photo from the Quality menu and select the type of printing paper you are using from the Paper type menu.

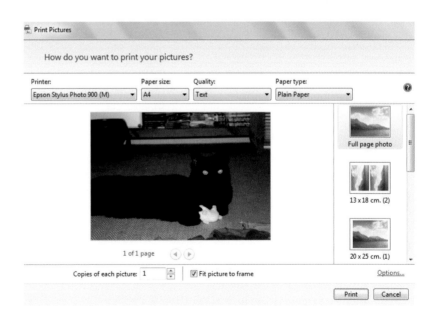

4 Click on the Print button to start printing

Ordering Prints

If you don't have a printer available, or you want to have your pictures professionally printed, Windows Photo Viewer has the ability to send your pictures directly to online companies. What happens is that you select an online company from a list of available companies, the pictures are uploaded to that company, you decide what you want to print and how many, then it's just a case of paying for them and they will be delivered to wherever you want.

To order your prints:

1 From the Print drop down box click on Order prints

2 Click on the printing company you want to use from the list of available companies

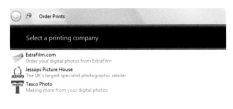

3 Click on Send Pictures

4 Confirm you want to send your pictures by clicking on the Send button

5 Follow through all the various steps with the printing company – these steps may include registering with the company, selecting various printing options and obviously paying for the prints

Don't forget

You must be connected to the Internet to order any prints. If you don't have an Internet connection available you could take your photos on a memory card or USB pen drive to have them printed somewhere.

177

Hot tip

Online companies also do more than just print your pictures onto paper – they often provide photo books, photos printed on T-shirts and much more.

Hot tip

Once you have used an online company you will have the option to use them again without having to go through the selection process again.

Tagging Pictures

You may have seen mention of the term 'tagging' in this book. You may also have seen the word Tags in the Pictures library.

Tagging is the term given to adding meaningful words or phrases to your pictures. These words and phrases could include what the picture is of, where it was taken, when it was taken and so on.

You can then easily sort and search your photos based on that tagging information.

To tag a picture:

1 From the Pictures library (or anywhere else you have your pictures) click on the picture you want to tag

2 At the bottom of the screen click on the Add a tag link

3 Type in the words or phrases that you want to use as the tag for that picture

4 When you have completed typing in the words or phrases click the Save button

Searching for Tagged Pictures

Once your pictures have been tagged, it is really easy to be able to find them again and display only those pictures you want.

For example, if you tagged some vacation photos with the location of your holiday, you can search for that location and anything with that place in the name or the tag will be displayed.

Type a word or phrase in the search box

13 Watching TV

This chapter will explain how to watch TV on your netbook and also about Windows Media Center, what it can do and how to use it.

Windows Media Center

Windows Media Center enables your netbook to be an all-in-one entertainment device that can sit in your living room, hotel room or anywhere else and provide all the benefits of a computer along with all the functionality of other devices such as stereos, DVD players and personal video recorders.

Don't forget

You don't have to use all the functionality of Windows Media Center if you don't want to. For example if you don't want or need to watch TV then you won't need a USB TV tuner card.

It has what is commonly referred to as "the ten foot interface" which basically means that you can use it and get all the benefits from it when you are sitting ten feet away on your couch because it has been specially designed to provide a different user experience to that of a normal computer. However you don't have to have it connected to a TV or other monitor, you can just watch it from your netbook screen and still enjoy all the benefits Windows Media Center has to offer.

Windows Media Center allows you to:

- Watch and record your favorite TV shows and movies
- Listen to music, CDs and even the radio
- Watch DVDs
- View slide shows of your photos and pictures
- Get access to exclusive online content
- Stream music and video to other rooms in your home using Windows Media Extenders such as an Xbox 360
- Synchronize your favorite contents to a portable Media Center device
- Search a 14-day TV guide and much more

Windows Media Center is the latest version in a long line of Media Center software from Microsoft and is included as a part of Windows 7 Home Premium, Professional and Ultimate.

Beware

While Windows Media Center will work on a netbook, it is designed to be run on more powerful hardware so you may want to just use some of the functionality.

There are a number of improvements over previous versions including:

- An improved user interface with easier navigation
- An Express Setup option to enable quicker first time use
- A new Mini guide when you are watching content

The User Interface

Access to the various features of Windows Media Center is through the main menu system which is controlled by either the remote control or via a mouse and keyboard.

There is a series of headings (such as TV, Movies, Music, etc.) and each one of those headings has a group of icons which control different elements within Windows Media Center.

To launch any of those elements is just a case of scrolling to the one you require and then selecting it.

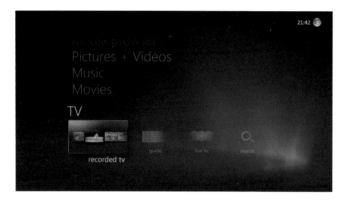

You can also control the shutdown functions for both Windows Media Center and Windows 7 itself from within the menu.

1   From the Tasks menu select Shutdown

2   You can choose from the following:

Close   Shut Down   Sleep

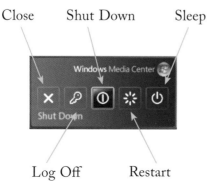

Log Off   Restart

The Remote Control

You can control Windows Media Center with a remote control which enables you to do everything from your couch.

There are different models available of the Windows Media Center remote control with a variety of different options.

As well as the remote control itself you will also need either an infrared receiver (IR) which is usually connected to your netbook via USB or a receiver that is built into the computer and may operate on a radio frequency or even via Bluetooth.

The prominent button on a Windows Media Center remote control is known as The Green Button. This button will actually launch Windows Media Center with a single touch.

Hot tip

The most enjoyable way to use Windows Media Center is with a remote control – this will mean connecting a USB remote receiver to your netbook. But don't worry if you don't want to use a remote, you can easily control Windows Media Center from the keyboard or mouse.

182

The remote may also have specific buttons that can perform the following type of functions:

- Navigation buttons for all types of playback including TV, movie and music

- One-touch recording

- Shortcuts for Pictures, TV, Music

- Volume controls and mute

- DVD menu

- A More button for additional menu options

- A button to launch the Guide

- Sleep which will put the Windows Media Center PC into hibernation

- Teletext quick buttons

- A number keypad that can also be used to enter text

Other Controls

If you don't have a remote control or you also want to control Windows Media Center in other ways you can use either the keyboard, a mouse or the on-screen controls.

Using a Mouse

You can launch Windows Media Center by using the mouse to select it from the Start Menu. You can then use the mouse to select menu items by clicking on them. If your mouse has a scroll wheel you can use it to scroll up and down through the menu. When you move the mouse the on-screen controls will appear if they are available.

You can then click any of these controls to activate them (such as channel - or +, play, pause or the volume controls).

Using a Keyboard

You can use a keyboard to control all of the features and functions of Windows Media Center either by using the arrow keys and ENTER or by using a variety of different keyboard shortcuts. Some of the more frequently used commands are:

Required Action	Keyboard shortcut
Launch Windows Media Center or return to the Start screen	Windows key + ALT + ENTER
Accept selection	ENTER
Go back to the previous screen	BACKSPACE
Go to Music	CTRL + M
Record a TV Show	CTRL + R
Launch the Guide	CTRL + G

Adding a TV Tuner

If you want to watch live TV or even record TV then you will need to connect a TV tuner to your netbook as you won't have one already built in. Fortunately these are now very small, and cheap, and can be connected to your netbook via a spare USB port. You will then need to connect an aerial into the tuner and then install any software and drivers in order for Windows Media Center to be able to use it.

To add a USB TV tuner to your netbook:

1. Connect the USB TV tuner to a spare port on your netbook

2. Install any software and drivers as directed

3. Connect an aerial to the tuner

Setting up Media Center

The first screen you will see after starting Windows Media Center for the first time is the initial welcome screen. From here you can decide whether to run Express setup, Custom setup or even Run setup later.

Express setup is the simplest and quickest way to get up and running with Windows Media Center. By selecting it Windows Media Center will automatically connect to the Internet to download any artwork and information on your media, and will also sign you up to the Customer Experience Improvement Program.

1 Click on the Start button

2 Click on Windows Media Center or All Programs and then Windows Media Center

3 Select which setup option you want to use by either using the remote control (if you have one connected), the keyboard or a mouse, ensuring the option is selected

4 Click on the option or press ENTER

Windows Media Center will now be configured and will be ready to use.

Hot tip

Unless you are really in a rush, always choose the Custom setup as it gives you more options to choose from.

185

Hot tip

You can run setup again at any time from Tasks, Settings, General, Windows Media Center Setup and selecting Run setup again. This will take you directly to Custom setup. If you want to see the initial setup again, just close Windows Media Center after selecting Run setup again and start it up again.

Watching TV

Windows Media Center enables you to watch TV and movies from the comfort of your sofa or armchair. You can watch live TV and even pause and rewind it without having previously set the show to record. You can choose to record a show or any program in a series, all with the touch of a button on the remote control.

Live TV

You can watch whatever TV show or movie is currently playing on any of the channels you can receive.

 1 Select Live TV from the TV + Movies menu

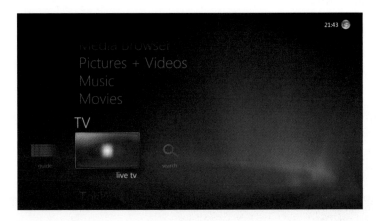

You will then see the first channel that is available along with any information provided by the Guide (such as program title, channel and its duration).

Hot tip

You can pause Live TV so that you don't miss anything if you get interrupted. You can then rewind and fast forward through the temporary recording.

Hot tip

You can also watch Live TV by pressing the Live TV button on the remote control – if you are using a remote control.

2 Use the Channel + and - buttons on the remote control to change the channel if needed

3 Press the More button on the remote control to display the options menu

Program Details
Record
Record Series
Search
View Categories
Edit Channel

Settings

These options include displaying program details, recording the program or any in the series, searching, viewing categories and other settings.

4 Select Program Details to see complete details on the show that is currently airing

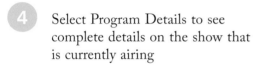

5 If you want to return to the show select Watch

Program information is also briefly displayed when changing channels.

Hot tip

You can quickly go to the last channel you were watching by pressing the Enter button on the remote control.

Don't forget

You can use your remote control to change the volume of whatever you are watching or even mute it if necessary.

Hot tip

You can use Teletext if it is available by either selecting Teletext from the Options menu or by pressing TXT on the remote control.

Internet TV

You don't need a TV tuner and an aerial source to watch TV on the Internet – all you need is an Internet connection.

Recently, more and more providers have been placing TV shows on the Internet for people to watch online. These providers include the actual TV stations themselves, like the BBC and ITV in the United Kingdom, and ABC and CBS in the United States.

To watch the shows all you need to do is to go to their website and choose what you want to watch.

There are also other services that have become very popular which enable you to watch content on your netbook. Two of the more popular services are the BBC iPlayer and Hulu.

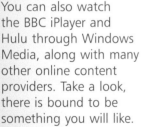

Don't forget

A lot of TV shows can only be watched in the country of origin due to copyright issues. So if you are in the UK, you will not be able to watch TV shows from US websites and vice versa.

Hot tip

You can also watch the BBC iPlayer and Hulu through Windows Media, along with many other online content providers. Take a look, there is bound to be something you will like.

BBC iPlayer

The BBC iPlayer enables you to watch content from the previous seven days via the website and to even download them to your netbook to watch later on the iPlayer Desktop software. There is a search function to help you locate what you want to watch as well. The iPlayer can be found at http://www.bbc.co.uk/iplayer.

Hulu

Hulu enables you to watch your favorite videos right from your browser, any time, for free. There are full episodes of TV shows both current and classic, full-length movies, web originals, and clips of just about everything. There are literally thousands of hours worth of things to watch so if you are in a hotel or you just want to watch something this might be for you.

14 Securing Your Netbook

This chapter will look at how you can protect your netbook and keep it secure, including looking at firewalls, passwords and physical security, plus keeping your netbook up to date and what to do if there is a problem.

Security Software

There are a number of threats on the Internet, or from other networks that you might connect your netbook to, which you really need to ensure you are protected against.

The easiest way to do this is to install some security software on your netbook. This software could include antivirus software, antispyware software, firewalls and other software.

There are many companies that produce security software, and this software ranges from free to chargeable, depending on what it is and who produces it. Add to this that some software requires a fee-based subscription to update what are known as definition files (the files that ensure the software knows all about the latest threats and how to deal with them) and you will need to make a decision on what to use.

Free Software
One thing you should keep in mind, just because something is free, doesn't mean it isn't any good. There are a number of free software products that you might want to consider, and here's a shortlist:

- Microsoft Security Essentials - http://www.microsoft.com/securityessentials

- AVG - http://www.avg.com (and search for AVG free)

Paid Software
There is also a lot of paid security software available, including:

- Norton AntiVirus and Norton Internet Security - http://www.norton.com

- McAfee VirusScan and McAfee Total Protection- http://www.mcafee.com

Netbook-Specific Software
Norton produce a Netbooks Edition of the Norton Internet Security suite. The software is not netbook specific but it does come on a USB stick for ease of installation for those people who don't have an external DVD drive.

Account Passwords

One of the simplest ways of protecting your netbook is to add a password to your Windows user account. This will stop someone from easily being able to access your files unless they know the password.

A password is something you have to type in so that you can gain access to your netbook – so think of it like a key to the door of your house. With the key you can get it, without the key you cannot.

Passwords should be difficult to guess, but should also be easy enough for you to remember. There is little point having a password that needs to be written down and kept with your netbook, so try to find that happy balance between difficult and memorable.

Password Do's and Don'ts

Here are some do's and don'ts when it comes to passwords:

- Do have a password on your netbook and on other services

- Do make it difficult to guess

- Do include both numbers and letters in the password, and possibly even other characters like - or !

- Do change your password on a regular basis

- Don't write your password down and keep it with your netbook

- Don't use the same password that you use on your other accounts – if someone guesses it then they will have access to every one of your accounts, and that is bad!

- Don't use obvious passwords like your birthday, or your children's names

- Don't use a short password – try to have at least 7 or 8 characters

- Don't EVER use a blank password or a password of PASSWORD

- Don't tell anyone your password – keep it a secret

Beware

Do not choose a password that is really easy to guess and do not write the password on a Post-it note and stick it on your netbook!

Hot tip

Use different passwords for different accounts – for example, use a different password for your Windows user account than that of your email account, and so on.

Setting a Password

If your Windows user account doesn't currently have a password associated with it, then now is a good time to add one.

To add a password to a Windows user account:

1 Ensure you are logged into the netbook with the user account that you want to set a password on

2 Click the Start button

3 Click on Control Panel

4 Click on User Accounts and Family Safety

User Accounts and Family Safety
Add or remove user accounts
Set up parental controls for any user

5 Click on Change your Windows password

 User Accounts
Change your account picture | Add or remove user accounts | Change your Windows password

6 Click on Create a password for your account

Make changes to your user account

Create a password for your account
Change your picture
Change your account name
Change your account type

Manage another account
Change User Account Control settings

Andrew Edney
Administrator

7 Type in the password in the box labeled New password, then type it again in the box labeled Confirm new password

Don't forget

From the User Account changes section you can also change your account name, account picture and even manage another Windows account if you have more than one on your netbook. For more information on these options take a look at Chapter 5.

8 If you want to have a hint available to you in case you forget your password, type it in the box labeled Type a password hint

Create a password for your account

Andrew Edney
Administrator

New password

Confirm new password

If your password contains capital letters, they must be typed the same way every time you log on.
How to create a strong password

Type a password hint

The password hint will be visible to everyone who uses this computer.
What is a password hint?

Create password   Cancel

Hot tip

Click on the How to create a strong password link for information and advice on creating strong passwords.

9 Click on the Create password button to finish creating the password and associating it with the selected user account

Now when you start your netbook you will be asked to enter a password before being allowed to go into Windows.

Beware

The password hint will be visible to anyone who uses your netbook so if you must use the password hint function try to make the hint something that only you would understand, and not something like "name of my cat", assuming that your password was the name of your cat.

Updating Windows

From time to time new software updates are released for Windows. These updates may include service packs that bring new functionality to Windows but more often than not they are security fixes and application patches.

It is very important to apply these fixes and patches as soon as possible because if it was important enough to release a fix then you will want to have that problem fixed as soon as you can so that you don't fall foul of the particular issue. For example, there might be a security flaw found in Internet Explorer which if left unfixed could enable someone to steal your bank account details and that would not be good.

To check to see if there are any updates and to update Windows:

1 Click on the Start button

2 Click on All Programs and then find and click on Windows Update

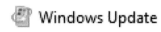

3 Click on the Check for updates button

Windows Update

Check for updates for your computer
Always install the latest updates to enhance your computer's security and performance.

Check for updates

Most recent check for updates: Never
Updates were installed: Today at 09:13. View update history
You receive updates: For Windows and other products from Microsoft Update

Find out more about free software from Microsoft Update. Click here for details.

Your netbook will now connect to the Windows Update service and see if there are any updates available. You may even see a message appear in the task tray telling you about new updates.

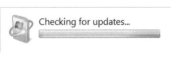
Checking for updates...

New updates are available
Click to install them using Windows Update.

...cont'd

4 You will see that there are a number of important updates that are available (these are always selected for you) and a few optional updates available. Click on optional updates to view what is available or skip to step 6

5 If you want to download and install any of the optional updates, just check the relevant box and then click OK

6 Click on the Install update button

The updates will now be downloaded one at a time and when they have all been downloaded they will then be installed for you. More often than not you will then need to restart your netbook.

7 Click the Restart now button to restart your netbook and complete the update process

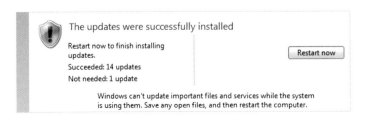

Beware

There are some optional updates that you can skip if you want, however you should never ever skip any security-related update as they are designed to keep you and your netbook safe.

Don't forget

Depending on how many updates there are available, how big they are and how fast your Internet connection is, this process can sometimes take a long time – so be patient.

195

System Restore

There may come a time when you install a new piece of software or hardware, or update existing software, and something goes wrong with the installation. What could happen then is that Windows stops working correctly or that application stops working correctly. The last thing you will want to do at this point is to have to reinstall Windows along with all your applications and everything else. Fortunately Windows comes with a feature known as System Restore.

System Restore helps you to restore your netbook's system files to an earlier point in time. None of your personal files such as your documents or photos will be changed, just the system files.

The way System Restore works is that restore points are created at different times, such as just before you install or update software and it is these restore points that are used to roll back to a previous state in the event of a problem.

To Recover Using System Restore
Using System Restore to recover to an earlier point is simply a case of selecting the required restore point:

1   Click on the Start Button and in the Search box type in System Restore

2   Click on System Restore from the results list

3   When System Restore starts, click the Next button

4   Scroll through the list of available restore points and click on the selected restore point

Don't forget

In order to recover to a previous restore point, that restore point must exist – so it may be useful to periodically create your own restore points in case you need them later, or just wait for automatic restore points to be created.

Don't forget

Save all of your files and close down any open applications before you start the system restore process.

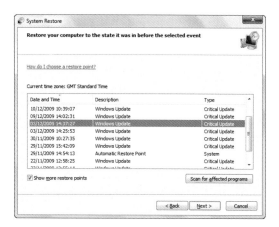

5 Click on the Next button

6 Confirm the restore point and click Finish to restore

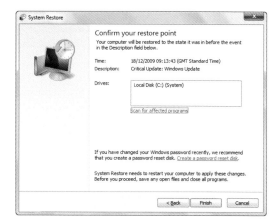

7 After your netbook has rebooted, click on the Close button and check to see if the problem has been resolved

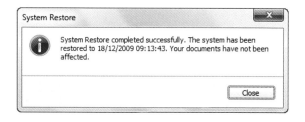

Don't forget

You will need to be connected to the Internet in order to check for, and download, any available updates from the Windows Update service.

Beware

If you decide not to use the Automatic Updates feature then you are leaving yourself open to possible problems with your netbook and you are relying on your memory to manually check for updates. Don't risk missing an important update – switch on Automatic Updates now!

Hot tip

The default settings for Automatic Updates include downloading and installing all recommended updates as well as important updates – this is useful so unless you really don't want to do this, leave the settings as they are.

Automatic Updates

Rather than having to manually check if there are any updates available, Windows provides a facility called Automatic Updates. What this does is to check if there are any updates for you at a predetermined time each day and if there are any updates available, download and install them automatically for you, depending on what you have selected to happen.

To turn on Automatic Updates:

1. Go to the Windows Update area and click on the Turn on automatic updates button

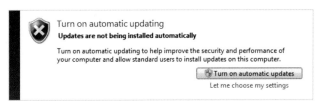

2. Click on the Let me choose my settings link if you want to make any changes to when and how the updates are performed and then click on the OK button to enable those changes

Choose how Windows can install updates

When your computer is online, Windows can automatically check for important updates and install them using these settings. When new updates are available, you can also install them before shutting down the computer.

How does automatic updating help me?

Important updates

Install updates automatically (recommended)

Install new updates: Every day at 03:00

Recommended updates

☑ Give me recommended updates the same way I receive important updates

Who can install updates

☑ Allow all users to install updates on this computer

Microsoft Update

☑ Give me updates for Microsoft products and check for new optional Microsoft software when I update Windows

Software notifications

☐ Show me detailed notifications when new Microsoft software is available

Note: Windows Update might update itself automatically first when checking for other updates. Read our

OK   Cancel

User Account Control

User Account Control is a feature of Windows that is designed to prevent potentially harmful programs from making changes to your netbook. For example, you don't want a program to try and disable your firewall so that an outside attacker on the Internet could gain access. The way that User Account Control works is that each time certain tasks are carried out, User Account Control will prompt you for permission. Unfortunately this can soon become very annoying and so you can set when these notifications take place. To see what the current level is set at and to change when to be notified:

Hot tip

When you first start using your netbook and installing new software and making configuration changes, you are likely to encounter UAC a lot – however, as time goes by and the changes become less frequent you will encounter UAC less, so just give it some time.

1 Click on the Start button and then Control Panel

2 Click on the User Accounts and Family Safety link

3 Click on the User Accounts link

4 Click on the Change User Account Control settings link

Change User Account Control settings

5 Use the slider to make changes to the UAC notification level and then click on OK

Hot tip

As you move the slider you can see what the notification level changes will actually mean to you – so read them carefully before making your final selection.

199

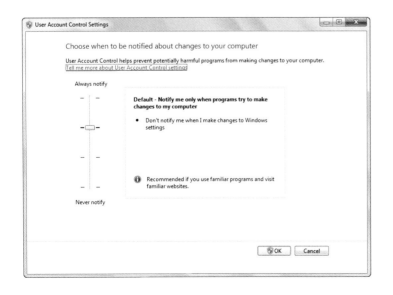

Beware

Don't be tempted to set the notification level to Never notify as this will mean that you will never know if changes are being made. While UAC can be a little annoying it is also there for a good reason so use it!

Security Essentials

Microsoft have introduced a free and easy to use antivirus and antispyware program called Security Essentials. If you didn't want to pay for a similar package then you could look at this.

To download and install Security Essentials:

1 Open your browser and go to http://www.microsoft.com/security_essentials

2 Click on the Download Now button and click on the Run button if you intend on installing the software once it has finished downloading

3 Follow the guided steps for installing Security Essentials

4 When the installation completes, ensure the Scan my computer box is checked and click the Finish button

You may want to have a look at, and change, some of the Security Essentials settings to suit your needs:

1 From the Security Essentials program, click on the Settings tab

2 You can change the settings by choosing new ones from the various drop down menus

3 Click the Save changes button when you are finished

Running a Scan

If you want to run a manual scan, and it is sensible to do so from time to time in case new definition files (the updates that tell Security Essentials about known viruses and spyware) pick anything up that was previously missed.

To run a manual scan:

1 From the Home tab, click on the scan option you want to run

2 Click on the Scan now button

3 Review the results and follow any instructions provided

Scan options:

- ⦿ Quick
- ⦾ Full
- ⦾ Custom...

[Scan now]

Windows Defender

Your netbook is also at risk from malware and spyware. Malware and spyware are also referred to as malicious software, which is basically any software that is doing something that you really don't want to be happening, such as recording what you do and where you visit on the Internet, placing pop-ups on your screen, allowing people to gain access to your netbook, and so on. There are a number of programs available that you could install in order to protect your netbook from malware, or you could just use Windows Defender which is built into Windows.

To Run a Scan With Windows Defender

It is a good idea to run a scan of your netbook regularly. To run a scan of your netbook using Windows Defender:

Don't forget

Windows comes with antimalware and antispyware software built in but it doesn't come with any antivirus so make sure that you install some immediately.

1 Click on the Start button

2 In the Search box type in Windows Defender

3 Click on Windows Defender from the displayed list

Windows Defender
Scan for spyware and other potentially unwanted software

4 If you are prompted, click on the Check for updates now button to ensure Windows Defender is up to date

Don't forget

You will need to be connected to the Internet to check for new definition files to update Windows Defender.

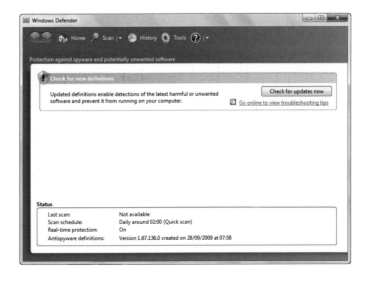

5 Click on the down arrow on the Scan button at the top of the screen

6 Click on the type of scan you want to run – if you are in a hurry just click on Quick scan

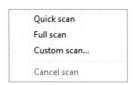

7 If the scan finds any problems you will be offered the choice of resolving them or reviewing them. If you want to resolve them click on the Clean system button but if you want to know more about it click on the review detected items link

8 Choose the action you want to take from the action list

9 Click on either the Clean system button or the Apply actions button to perform the required action

Don't forget

Make sure that you keep Windows Defender up to date so that you are protected as much as possible. Windows Defender is updated using Windows Update or is done for you if you have enabled Automatic Updates.

Hot tip

If you are in a hurry you can choose the Quick scan option, but to ensure you are fully checked you should try and find the time to perform a Full scan of your netbook.

Beware

If Windows Defender finds a problem then you should really trust it and either remove it or if you are not sure you can quarantine it.

Windows Firewall

You may have heard of firewalls. A firewall is a piece of software (or hardware if you have purchased something more elaborate and expensive) that is used to prevent unauthorized access to your netbook and network from any external source.

Usually, firewalls block everything and only allow what you instruct them to allow through. These allowances are known as exceptions. The idea being that if you have not explicitly allowed in something that you know about, then it stays out.

Windows has a built-in firewall that should be sufficient for most people to use. You can of course go and buy another firewall and install it instead of using the Windows firewall – the choice is yours, just make sure whichever one you choose is easy to use.

To check the status of the Windows Firewall:

Beware

Never connect to the Internet unless you have got some sort of firewall running on your netbook otherwise you risk your netbook being attacked and compromised and then your data will not be safe.

1 Click on the Start button

2 Click on the Control Panel button

3 Click on System and Security

System and Security
Review your computer's status
Back up your computer
Find and fix problems

4 Click on Windows Firewall

Don't forget

The Windows Firewall is already switched on and is protecting you without the need for you to do anything extra to be protected.

204

Windows Firewall
Check firewall status | Allow a program through Windows Firewall

Don't forget

"Connected" refers to the fact that you are connected to that specific network type.

From the Windows Firewall screen you can easily see if the
Windows Firewall is enabled (it's the Windows Firewall
state) and other information. You will also be able to see this
information for both the Home and Work networks (also referred
to as Private networks – these are the networks you trust, for
example your home network) and also any Public networks (such
as ones you might use in an Internet cafe (which you shouldn't
trust quite as much as your home network).

Modifying the Windows Firewall

You can modify the settings for the Windows Firewall, for
example you might want to turn it off in favor of using a different
firewall. To make changes to the Windows Firewall:

1 From the Windows Firewall,
click on the Change
notification settings link on
the left hand of the screen

2 Make any changes you want to the Windows Firewall
– for example, if you wanted to turn off the Windows
Firewall you just need to click the Turn off Windows
Firewall radio button

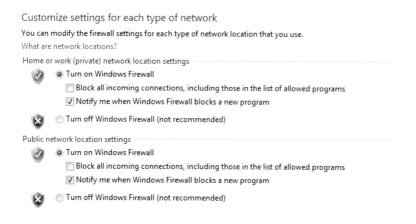

3 Click on the OK button to save your changes

...cont'd

Allowing Programs Through the Windows Firewall

You may find that you have a need to allow a program or a Windows feature through the firewall that is not allowed by default.

To allow or disallow a program through the Windows Firewall:

1. From the Windows Firewall click on the Allow a program or feature through Windows Firewall link on the left hand side of the screen

Allow a program or feature through Windows Firewall

2. Click on the Change settings button

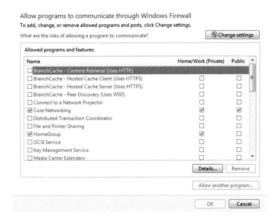

3. Scroll through the list of programs and features shown and make your changes

4. Click OK to save the changes

You may also be prompted to allow an application through the Windows firewall when you install something – this is certainly easier than adding an application manually!

The Action Center – Security

The Action Center is a central place to view alerts and to take actions that can help keep your netbook running smoothly.

To view the security elements of the Action Center:

1 Click the Start button and then Control Panel

2 Click on System and Security

3 Click on Action Center

Action Center
Review your computer's status and resolve issues
Change User Account Control settings | Troubleshoot common computer problems
Restore your computer to an earlier time

4 Click on Security to expand the list and if anything needs actioning click on the relevant buttons to perform the actions if you decide that is what you want to do

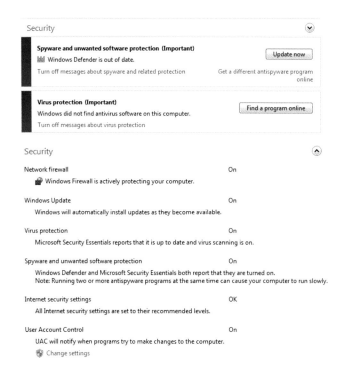

Security ⌄

Spyware and unwanted software protection (Important)
Windows Defender is out of date.   [Update now]
Turn off messages about spyware and related protection   Get a different antispyware program online

Virus protection (Important)
Windows did not find antivirus software on this computer.   [Find a program online]
Turn off messages about virus protection

Security ⌃

Network firewall   On
Windows Firewall is actively protecting your computer.

Windows Update   On
Windows will automatically install updates as they become available.

Virus protection   On
Microsoft Security Essentials reports that it is up to date and virus scanning is on.

Spyware and unwanted software protection   On
Windows Defender and Microsoft Security Essentials both report that they are turned on.
Note: Running two or more antispyware programs at the same time can cause your computer to run slowly.

Internet security settings   OK
All Internet security settings are set to their recommended levels.

User Account Control   On
UAC will notify when programs try to make changes to the computer.
Change settings

Don't forget

Even though the Security list in the Action Center may not show any buttons, there may be information that is useful, such as the warning about both Windows Defender and Microsoft Security Essentials both running at the same time.

Physical Security

Just as important as protecting your netbook with updates and antivirus software is physical security. It's all well and good making sure your netbook is protected when it is running, but what good is that if someone just steals the netbook from you?

There are some very easy and cheap ways of protecting your netbook.

Kensington Locks
Most netbooks have a little slot on the side of them, often shown next to a picture of a padlock with a K on it. This is called a Kensington lock port and you can use a Kensington lock to protect your netbook from theft by attaching one end of the lock to something stationary, like a table, and the other end connects to the Kensington lock port on the netbook. This should deter most opportunistic thieves from stealing your netbook while you are not looking, or if you need to step away from where you are using your netbook.

Bag Protection
In order to stop someone from easily opening your bag and removing your netbook without your knowledge you could buy yourself a small combination padlock that is designed specifically for use on bags.

Protecting Your External Data Devices
Any external data device you use, such as an external hard drive or a USB drive, needs to be protected. After all, they may contain some of your sensitive data and are very easy to drop or leave somewhere by accident. Always check that you have them with you and don't leave them out in the open where they could be easily stolen without you realizing it.

Beware

No lock is 100% foolproof so the safest way to ensure your netbook is not stolen is to never leave it anywhere – just take it with you if you need to leave the place where you are working.

Hot tip

Never leave your bag unattended at any time. A lock is useful but if a potential thief just steals your bag with the netbook in it they can easily gain access to the bag whenever they want.

S

T

U